Diane Warner's

Contemporary Guide to

WEDDING

ETIQUETTE

**Advice From America's Most
Trusted Wedding Expert**

 A div
Frank

DIANE WARNER'S CONTEMPORARY GUIDE TO WEDDING ETIQUETTE
EDITED AND TYPESET BY KATE HENCHES
Cover design by DesignConcept
Printed in the U.S.A. by Book-mart Press

To order this title, please call toll-free 1-800-CAREER-1 (NJ and Canada: 201-848-0310) to order using VISA or MasterCard, or for further information on books from Career Press.

The Career Press, Inc., 3 Tice Road, PO Box 687,
Franklin Lakes, NJ 07417
www.careerpress.com
www.newpagebooks.com

Library of Congress Cataloging-in-Publication Data

Warner, Diane.
    Diane Warner's contemporary guide to wedding etiquette : advice from America's most trusted wedding expert / by Diane Warner.
        p. cm.
    Includes index.
    ISBN 1-56414-761-4 (pbk.)
    1. Wedding etiquette. I. Title.

BJ2051.W265 2005
395.2'2--dc22

2004048620

DEDICATION

I dedicate this book to my precious niece,
Carrie Anne.

Acknowledgments

I have so many people to thank. First of all, thank you Michael Pye, Assistant Acquisitions Editor, who decided I should write this book. My thanks also go to other important people at Career Press/New Page Books: Michael Lewis, Senior Acquisitions Editor; Kirsten Beucler, Marketing Coordinator; Adam Schwartz, Sales Assistant; and my editor, Kate Henches.

I also appreciate the help and advice of my agent, Jeff Herman, and, finally, my thanks go to three wonderful women who agreed to review my manuscript before it went to publication: Sharon Elaine Lewis, Publisher and Executive Producer of *Washington Weddings* Magazine and *The Wedding Show* in Washington, D.C.; Doris M. Nixon, President, Weddings Beautiful Worldwide, a division of National Bridal Service; and Mimi Doke, CSEP, MBC, The Wedding Specialist, Lake Havasu City, Arizona.

CONTENTS

INTRODUCTION

Planning a wedding is an enormous undertaking. In fact, some say a wedding is as complicated to put together as a large theater production. There is one major difference, however: a wedding must be planned according to rules of etiquette.

Wedding etiquette is defined as "the practices and forms prescribed by social convention and authority" as they pertain to a wedding (*American Heritage College Dictionary*). In other words, etiquette is a set of rules that should be followed, in the same way you must play by the rules in any game. For example, in the game of golf, you're required to play by the strict rules dictated by the United States Golf Association (USGA) in their little rule book. The USGA has rules for everything, including the size of the golf ball, how many golf clubs you're allowed to carry in your bag, and which player should putt first on the green.

Always followed in a professional golf tournament, these strict rules of golf are comparable to the traditional rules of wedding etiquette, which are usually followed for a formal or ultraformal wedding.

In today's world of less formal weddings, however, couples prefer to bend the rules, depending on their wedding's degree of informality. This contemporary spin can be compared to a less formal game of golf where a foursome plays a casual, friendly game and takes all kinds of liberties. For example, a player may be encouraged to "just kick it out of the rough, Fred," an action which is known in golf circles as a *foot wedgie*. Or, if a golfer doesn't like his drive, he can take a mulligan—golf jargon for a "do-over."

If you're planning a very formal wedding, you'll probably choose to follow the rules precisely. However, even if you're planning an informal wedding, you should be familiar with the rules before you decide how far to bend them. You'll also find that certain rules *must* be followed for all weddings, even a super-casual wedding on the beach, because you don't want to damage precious relationships or hurt anyone's feelings. We'll talk more about this throughout the book as we apply the rules to these five degrees of formality:

Ultraformal

- A minimum of 200 guests.
- Held at an upscale venue, such as a cathedral, synagogue, resort, or country club.
- Ten or more total attendants.
- Elegant sit-down dinner and a ballroom for dancing to live music.

Formal

- A minimum of 100 guests.
- Held at an upscale site, similar to an ultraformal wedding.
- Six or more total attendants.

- Sit-down or buffet dinner.
- Live music or DJ.

Semiformal

- Fewer than 100 guests.
- Held in a church, home, outdoors, or other less formal setting.
- Two or more attendants.
- Light lunch or finger food reception.
- Live music or DJ.

Informal

- Fewer than 50 guests.
- Held in a chapel, a home, or other informal setting.
- Two attendants: maid or matron of honor and best man.
- Light breakfast, brunch, finger food, or dessert-only reception.

Casual

Many of today's weddings can be considered casual, such as one that takes place on horseback, at the top of a ski slope, or during a beach party where everyone, including the bride and groom, wear swimsuits.

How formal will your wedding be? Will you need to follow the rules to the letter? Or, will you be allowed to bend the rules with a few *foot wedgies* and *mulligans*? In any case, this book will lay out all the rules and their contemporary alternatives.

Traditional or contemporary—the choice is up to you.

Chapter 1

THE ENGAGEMENT SEASON

You auditioned for the part and you got it! Your fiancé chose you to play his leading lady in the biggest production of your lives. Your engagement season will be an enchanting time for you as you try out your new roles and become the center of attention at parties and celebrations.

A certain amount of traditional etiquette comes into play when you become engaged, especially concerning such things as who to tell first, how to introduce your parents to his parents, when to announce your engagement in the newspaper, and what's expected during the pre-wedding festivities.

Telling Your Parents

Your parents are the first people you should tell that you've become engaged, preferably in person. Traditional engagement etiquette dictates that you inform the bride's parents first. However, according to contemporary etiquette, it really doesn't matter, just as long as both sets of parents hear about it before anyone else. If your parents are divorced, of course, you'll be making several telephone calls.

Occasionally, the groom follows the old-fashioned custom of asking the bride's father for permission to marry her.

In fact, our son-in-law invited my husband out to lunch, during which he asked for permission to marry our daughter. Of course, my husband said yes. Not only did we already love and respect him, but we definitely saw it coming. This tradition isn't usually followed in today's contemporary world of etiquette because the decision is considered to be up to the couple themselves.

Introducing the Two Sets of Parents

The groom's parents should contact the bride's parents to arrange a meeting. It doesn't matter where they get together, although a private home is usually a warm and fuzzy choice. In the case of our daughter and her fiancé, his parents lived about 90 miles away, so they called us to arrange a meeting in a restaurant midway between our two cities. In our case, our daughter and their son were with us, but it's fine for the parents to meet without their children present.

If either of your parents are divorced and can't stand to be in the same room at the same time, it will be necessary to meet each parent separately. For example, the bride's parents (who are not divorced) may meet with the groom's mother for lunch one day, then with his father for cocktails on another occasion.

When the Parents Don't Approve of the Marriage

It's unfortunate when one or both sets of parents don't approve of the marriage, but it's still a good idea to try to get them together for a cordial meeting. Usually, a disgruntled parent will bite his or her tongue and go along with the plans.

If your parents not only disapprove of the marriage, but also refuse to attend the wedding or contribute toward the expenses, plan the wedding on your own with whatever funds you can scrape together. However, out of respect for your parents, send them a wedding invitation anyway.

Telling Other Relatives

Now the fun begins—you get to tell the rest of your relatives, including Grandpa and Grandma, all your aunts, uncles, cousins, and, of course, your siblings. You may decide to make a surprise announcement during a family get-together, or you can let each person know, individually, in person or with a telephone call.

Telling Your Friends

After you've dutifully notified your parents and other relatives, you can finally let the news out of the bag. Tell your closest friends first, in person if possible. Then, you can let the rest of your world know through telephone calls, personal contact or—and this is fun—by just happening to wear your new sparkling diamond to work, church, or some other get-together.

Your Engagement Portrait

Once you've told everyone the good news, it's time to arrange for your engagement portrait, which you may want included in your newspaper announcement. Traditional etiquette dictated that only the bride was photographed for the engagement portrait, but contemporary etiquette allows for you and your fiancé to be photographed together.

The engagement portrait is usually photographed by your wedding photographer, so you'll need to hire this professional right away.

Once you've chosen your photographer, you'll need to decide on the formality of your portrait. The trend is toward casual, informal engagement portraits, often in outdoor settings. Ask to see examples of the various styles offered by your photographer.

> Although the average engagement lasts 15 months, it's proper to send your announcement to the newspaper as soon as possible after you've become engaged.

Newspaper Announcement

Once you have your engagement portrait, it's time to send it and your official engagement announcement to your local newspaper. If you're attending college in a certain town, but each of you is from a different city, send announcements to all three newspapers. Call the newspapers and find out what they require. They will mail or fax you a form to fill out. If they don't, you can send them the engagement photo, along with pertinent information, including your names, occupations, schools attended, your parents' names and home towns, and when you plan to be married.

The bride's parents usually make the announcement or, in the case of divorced parents, the bride's mother or father may do so. If the bride's parents are deceased, another relative may make the announcement, or the couple may announce their own engagement.

The following is traditional wording when the bride's parents are making the announcement:

Dr. and Mrs. James Ketterson of Elgin, Arizona
announce the engagement of their daughter,
Katrina Marie, to Mr. Austin Monroe,
the son of Mr. and Mrs. Robert Monroe of Miami, Florida

If the bride's parents are divorced, this wording may be used:

Mrs. Esther Irving announces the engagement of her daughter,
Miss Sandra Lynn Irving to Blake Tennington,
the son of Mr. and Mrs. Roger Tennington.
Miss Irving is also the daughter of Mr. Conrad Irving of San Mateo, California

If the couple is announcing their own engagement, this wording may be used:

Miss Sandra Irving and Mr. Blake Tennington
are pleased to announce their engagement

> Sorry, but even contemporary etiquette considers it poor taste to announce your engagement via e-mail!

Engagement Parties

You may be honored with several parties, hosted by parents, relatives, or friends. It may be an announcement party, where your engagement is announced for the first time. Or, it may be one of several engagement celebrations.

Engagement Party Etiquette

Engagement parties usually take place as soon as possible after the couple becomes engaged. The important thing to remember is that these parties shouldn't crowd any pre-wedding festivities, especially if it is to be a short engagement period. Gifts aren't required, although they are usually given during a family party.

A few important rules of etiquette for a formal engagement party:

- ∞ The bride and groom must attend all engagement parties together.

- ∞ Everyone invited to an engagement party must also be invited to the wedding.

- ∞ The party should be tasteful. For example, it would be in poor taste to give the bride intimate lacy negligees, or the groom something risqué that would be more appropriate for a bachelor party.

- ∞ Appropriate engagement gifts may be precious family heirlooms being handed down by a relative, or sentimental gifts that will be treasured for many years, such as an elegantly framed engagement photo or a pillow embroidered with the couple's wedding date.

- ∞ If only a few of the guests bring gifts, don't open them during the party, because this may embarrass those who didn't. Open the gifts after all the guests have left.

- ∞ A formal engagement party requires that the invitation be engraved or handwritten by a calligrapher. A less formal party invitation may be computer-generated, handwritten, or extended by telephone or fax.

It's a good idea to establish gift registries before engagement parties take place. Although gifts aren't required for an engagement party, certain friends and family members may want to present the couple with a gift, and a registry makes it easier for them to decide what to buy. Establishing several gift registries isn't considered greedy, but actually provides a service to potential gift givers, not only for engagement parties, but wedding showers and the wedding itself (see Chapter 3).

Announcement Party

An engagement party that takes place soon after the couple becomes engaged may serve as a convenient *announcement party*, as friends and relatives hear of your engagement for the first time. This party may be hosted by the couple's parents, their friends, or themselves. It may become a surprise party as the engagement is announced during some other occasion, such as a singles' Valentine's or New Year's Party, a family reunion, or a Christmas party.

Engagement Celebration

Once the engagement has officially been announced, anyone may host an engagement celebration—office employees, church friends, college buddies, or new friends you've made through your line dance class or travel club.

The party may be formal or informal, although a party hosted by family members is usually more on the formal side, such as an elegant sit-down dinner or a romantic dessert party.

Or, it may lean toward the informal with a country-western barbecue, an Hawaiian luau, or an old-fashioned meet-the-family picnic.

The Engagement Ring and Other Wedding Jewelry

An engagement is official with or without an engagement ring, although, traditionally, the man presents the woman with a diamond ring when he asks her to marry him.

Although approximately 70 percent of today's brides receive a diamond engagement ring, there are many lovely, acceptable options:

- An heirloom ring from the groom's family (or an heirloom stone placed in a new setting).

- A synthetic "diamond" ring (to be replaced by the real thing at a later date).

- A cultured pearl, sapphire, or ruby ring.

- A ring set with the woman's birthstone.

- A diamond engagement bracelet or a diamond heart on a gold chain necklace.

The jewelry industry has come up with a rule that says the man should spend two months' salary on his intended's engagement ring. Use this rule as a guideline, but spend only what you can afford. Also, look for a reputable jeweler who is a member of the American Gem Society, a professional organization that prides itself on its high ethical standards.

Often a couple shops together for the engagement ring and their wedding bands. In fact, only about a third of the men buy the engagement ring without input from their girlfriends. The bride's and groom's bands may or may not match. Traditionally, the bride pays for her groom's wedding ring and vice versa.

One of today's contemporary twists is for the bride's engagement ring to serve double duty as her engagement and wedding ring. If you like this option, she may wear the ring before the wedding as an engagement ring, but remove it before the ceremony so that her groom may present it to her again, this time as her wedding ring.

Many couples have their wedding bands engraved before the wedding. The most popular choice is to have the rings inscribed with the couple's initials and the wedding date, although personalized phrases may be inscribed instead, such as a certain verse of scripture.

> In the case of a broken engagement, the engagement ring should be returned to her ex-fiancé, unless he died, in which case the bride may keep the ring. If the ring was a treasured heirloom from his side of the family, it should be returned, however.

Chapter 2

MONEY MATTERS

Every show needs backers who are willing to invest in the production. Of course, anyone investing in a wedding doesn't expect a financial return.

Traditional etiquette dictates that the bride's parents pay for most of the wedding expenses, while the groom's parents pay for the rehearsal dinner and a few other costs. In today's world, however, with weddings averaging about $22,000, it has become a joint effort to pay for the wedding. In other words, you need more than one producer for this show. Each set of parents usually contributes as much as they can afford, with the balance being picked up by other relatives and the couple themselves. In fact, 40 percent of today's couples pay for all their wedding costs, especially those who are well-established in their careers.

If your parents agree to help out with the expenses, but you have your heart set on an elaborate wedding that your parents can't begin to afford, they shouldn't be expected to mortgage their home to pay for your wedding. In fact, according to contemporary etiquette, whatever they contribute should be considered a gift, and the remaining expenses are your responsibility.

The best option for everyone involved is to plan an affordable wedding, which *is* possible to do, as several of my books explain, including *How to Have a Big Wedding on a Small Budget, 4th Edition* (Betterway Books, 2002). You'll find that you can actually cut costs in many ways without cutting quality.

When Money Isn't a Factor

Some families are financially able to pay for the wedding according to the traditional rules of etiquette. If this is true of your family, here is the customary breakdown of expenses for each party:

Traditional Expenses of the Bride's Family

- Family engagement party.
- Wedding gown and trousseau.
- Cost of a wedding coordinator, if one is hired.
- Wedding invitations, announcements, ceremony programs, and all other printed materials.
- Rental of the ceremony and reception sites.
- Decoration of both sites.
- Fees for the musicians.
- Transportation of the bridesmaids to the ceremony and reception.
- Entire cost of the reception, including the cake, food, beverages, caterer's fees, gratuities, and so forth.
- All photography and videography, including the bride's engagement photograph.

- Lodging for all out-of-town bridesmaids and the bride's relatives.

- Gift baskets for out-of-town guests.

- Gifts for the bridesmaids and other helpers.

- All flowers (except for those worn by the bride, groom, groomsmen, parents, and grandparents.)

- Groom's wedding ring and wedding gift from the bride.

> It's a good idea to have one person in charge of the budget, including the inflow and outflow of the money, and how much money is still available in each category. Assign this duty to someone who is highly organized, the type of person who enjoys balancing the checkbook and gets a kick out of doing income taxes.

Traditional Expenses of the Groom's Family

- The bride's rings.

- The marriage license.

- The officiant's fee.

- Rehearsal dinner/party.

- Groom's wedding attire.

- Lodging for the out-of-town groomsmen and the groom's relatives.

- Gift baskets for out-of-town guests.

- Gifts for the best man, groomsmen, and ushers.

- Boutonnieres for the groom, the best man, the groom's attendants, and both fathers and grandfathers.

- The bride's bouquet and going-away corsage.

- Corsages for both mothers and all grandmothers.

- The honeymoon.

> If either set of parents pays for most of the wedding, this does not give them the right to *plan* the wedding. Regardless of who is paying for the wedding, this is *your* wedding, not your mother's wedding, not your Aunt Hester's wedding. So, as kindly as possible, thank everyone for their financial contributions, but make it clear that you and your fiancé will be making the major planning decisions. If this isn't well accepted, you may need to turn down their financial help, even if it means planning a less elaborate wedding you can afford from your own funds.

Traditional Expenses of the Bridal Attendants

- Their own attire.

- Transportation to and from the city where the wedding will take place.

- Shared expenses of a bridal shower and/or bachelorette party.

- Gifts for the bridal shower.

- Joint wedding gift.

Traditional Expenses of the Groom's Attendants

- ∞ Their own attire.

- ∞ Transportation to and from the city where the wedding will take place.

- ∞ Shared expenses of the bachelor party.

- ∞ Joint wedding gift.

Don't forget to add in the cost of gratuities. Although tipping isn't required, it is an expected reward for excellent service.

Guidelines for Tipping

Caterers and/or waitstaff:	15 to 20%
Parking valet:	$1.50 per guest
Coat or restroom attendant:	$ .50 per guest
Limousine drivers:	15 to 20%
DJs:	15 to 20%
Band:	$20 per band member

Some of your vendors may include gratuities in their invoices, so watch for that. Also, it's not customary to tip anyone who is being paid a flat fee, such as your florist or pastry chef.

Chapter 3

The Gift Registries

A gift registry is a wish list established at a variety of stores by the bride and groom so that friends and relatives will know what the couple wants as wedding gifts. When we were kids, we sat on Santa's knee and told him what we wanted for Christmas. When Christmas morning finally dawned, however, our requested gifts weren't always under the Christmas tree. So disappointing! You won't be disappointed, however, by establishing wedding gift registries, because people actually buy the items you've requested.

Enjoy your 15 minutes of fame and establish gift registries all over town! After all, how many times in your life will you have adoring fans throwing gifts at the feet of the star?

Traditional Etiquette

Traditionally, the bride registers at an upscale department or specialty store for her choices of linen, china, crystal, silver, cookware, and so forth. The registry is offered by these stores as a free service, along with the guidance of a professional wedding gift consultant who will help the bride make her selections.

Many stores provide the bride with a scanner, so she can easily scan the code attached to any gift in the store. Once the registry is established, the computerized registry keeps close tabs on which gifts have been purchased and those that are still available for purchase.

> When registering, always include the bride's or her parents' home address, so that gifts may be delivered directly. It is poor taste for a gift to be brought to the ceremony or reception, although this is actually commonplace.

In addition to registering at local stores, the bride can also register with national chains online, which is a great convenience for out-of-town guests. Whether you register at a local store or online, you'll find a list of suggested gifts. For example, they'll tell you how many pieces should be included in each place setting of flatware, glassware, and china.

Contemporary Options

Contemporary registries are a lot more fun than traditional registries because they offer a wider variety of gifts in many price ranges. Most of these gifts are selected by the bride and groom together. For example, the couple may register for:

- Camping or mountaineering equipment.
- Gardening supplies.
- Chain saw.

- Lawn mower.

- A down payment on a home—register with a mortgage company.

- A honeymoon—register with a travel agency.

- Furniture—register with a furniture store.

- Art—register with an art gallery.

If your fiancé isn't excited about going with you to set up gift registries, don't worry about it. Take along your mom or your best friend for advice and establish the registries yourself. With today's contemporary choices, however, most men get a kick out of registering for something they understand, like a power drill.

Frequently Asked Questions About Wedding Gifts

When should we register?

Register as soon as you become engaged. Although guests aren't *required* to purchase gifts through one of these registries, at least the registries are established and available for anyone who does choose to use them. These registries will come in handy for anyone purchasing a gift for an engagement party, a wedding shower, or, of course, the wedding itself.

Can we list a few highly priced items, or should the gifts be within a certain price range?

The gifts should be in a variety of price ranges, which will allow your guests a choice. It's best, however, not to list too many high-priced gifts because you don't want your guests to feel guilty if they can only afford something less pricey. It's common for several friends, relatives, or coworkers to go together to purchase the more expensive gifts on your list.

How long should we keep the registries open after the wedding?

Technically, according to traditional etiquette, a wedding gift may be purchased up to a year after the wedding. However, most people purchase wedding gifts as close to the wedding date as possible.

Is it all right to list a few of our gift registries on the bottom of our wedding invitation?

No—baaaaad taste! It *is* okay, however, to "get the word out." You'll find that guests may ask you in person or call your parents to find out where you're registered. You may list your gift registries in your wedding newsletter or on your wedding Website, should you choose to have either.

What if gifts arrive damaged or broken?

If you know where a gift was purchased, take it back to the store and ask for a replacement.

> *Don't let the donor know the gift arrived damaged if you can help it, but write a lovely thank-you note and don't breathe a word about it. Only when a broken or damaged gift arrives fully insured should you contact the giver.*

What if we receive duplicate gifts?

Exchange one of them for something else, but don't let the donors know. Write each a thank-you note, as if their gift was the one-and-only of its kind.

> If you receive a gift you just don't like and you know you'll never use, such as a bright red and green ceramic rooster, think twice before exchanging it for something else. Will the giver ever be a guest in your home and notice that their gift is missing from your kitchen counter? Or, is the gift from a distant third cousin you haven't seen in 20 years? In the latter case, take the darned thing back and exchange it—that is, if you know where it was purchased. Otherwise, keep the rooster handy and if you see the giver driving up your driveway, yank it out of the cupboard and display it on your kitchen counter!

What about re-gifting duplicate gifts or gifts we don't like?

Although re-gifting (converting a gift you received into a future wedding or bridal shower gift for someone else) is common practice , it's risky business. What if you accidentally give a friend the exact same gift she gave you for your bridal shower? She'll recognize it, I guarantee you, so unless you concoct some kind of clever system to keep track of who gave you what, you're in danger of hurting someone's feelings.

If the wedding is canceled for some reason, are we required to return the wedding gifts?

Absolutely! Not only should they be returned, but they should be accompanied by a personal note, if possible. Usually the bride writes notes to her friends and family members, and the groom to his. Here is sample wording:

Dear Jim and Hazel,

Unfortunately, Joe and I have canceled our wedding. We are returning the lovely linen tablecloth you sent us. Thank you for your thoughtfulness.

Love,
Leigh Anne

Never ask guests for their gift receipts so you can exchange their gifts. If you can't exchange a gift without a receipt, forget it. After all, what if the gift was something the giver received at *her* wedding and *she's* re-gifting it to you? Or, what if she bought it at a flea market or garage sale?

Chapter 4

Your Cast of Characters

A wedding is an enormous production that requires a large cast of characters, including the bride, the groom, parents, attendants, flower girl, ring bearer, candlelighters, helpers, and any children from previous marriages. People problems and strained relationships can be avoided by following a few sensible rules of wedding etiquette. In fact, traditional and contemporary rules of etiquette are pretty much the same when dealing with the members of your wedding party. For example, even over-the-top casual weddings still require a certain protocol to avoid hurt feelings. People can be fragile beings, and they must be handled with care.

First of all, the rules of proper etiquette must be followed as you select the members of your wedding party. They should also be followed when it comes to each person's responsibilities, including the bride and groom. In order to adhere to proper wedding etiquette, everyone must accomplish their tasks in a logical order. This chapter includes guidelines for choosing the members of your cast, plus a list of responsibilities for each cast member.

We'll begin with the most important members of the cast.

The Leading Man and Leading Lady

The starring roles are played by the bride and groom. Without them, the production can't go on!

The Bride

The bride is the brightest star in the show and everyone looks to her for direction. Does she want a large wedding or a small wedding? Does she want her wedding to be formal or informal? Indoors or outdoors? What type of gown will she choose?

As the bride makes these decisions, she'll consult with her leading man and the members of her supporting cast. Here are some of her important responsibilities:

- Makes the major decisions regarding the wedding's size and formality.
- Sets up a wedding budget, based on how much money everyone is able to contribute, including family members and the bride and groom themselves.
- Sets the date and time of the wedding.
- Helps compose the guest list.
- Chooses her wedding attendants (including flower girls) and arranges lodging for those who don't live locally.
- Meets with the ceremony officiant and receives premarital counseling, if she and her fiancé decide to take advantage of this privilege.
- Purchases her gown and decides on her attendants' attire.

- Interviews wedding vendors and service providers.
- Solicits help from friends and family members, then delegates responsibilities.
- Chooses her ceremony and reception sites.
- Shops for a wedding cake.
- Decides on dozens of details regarding the ceremony and reception, including decorations, flowers, music, and reception food.
- Shops with her groom for wedding rings and decides on inscriptions, if desired.
- Purchases a wedding gift for her groom.
- Updates her passport, if required for honeymoon travel.
- Shops for thank-you gifts for her parents, her attendants, and those who are helping with the wedding.
- Plans a bridesmaids' tea or luncheon, unless her honor attendant and bridesmaids have planned this event.
- Stands in the receiving line, if she chooses to have one.
- Dances the first dance with the groom, followed by dancing with her father, the groom's father, and the best man.
- Offers a toast to her groom during the reception (optional).
- Writes personal thank-you notes for every wedding gift received before, during, and after the wedding.

The Groom

The groom is the co-star of the show and, along with his leading lady, helps make important decisions regarding the wedding's formality, size, and style. As a matter of fact, today's groom is more involved in the wedding plans than ever before. Here are some of his important responsibilities:

- Helps set up a wedding budget, based on the total funds available.
- Helps compose the guest list.
- Chooses his groomsmen and ushers and arranges lodging for any who don't live locally.
- Chooses the ring bearer.
- Meets with the ceremony officiant and receives premarital counseling, if he and his bride decide to take advantage of this privilege.
- Arranges for the rental of his and his attendants' wedding attire.
- Helps his bride interview wedding vendors and service providers.
- Arranges a date to obtain the marriage license.
- Plans the honeymoon and makes sure he and his bride have current passports, if required.
- Orders and pays for the wedding flowers that are his responsibility.
- Shops with his bride for wedding rings and decides on the inscriptions, if desired.
- Purchases a wedding gift for his bride.
- Shops for thank-you gifts for his parents and his attendants.

- Stands in the receiving line with his bride, if there is one.
- Dances the first dance with his bride, followed by dancing with his mother, the bride's mother, and the bride's honor attendant.
- During the reception, he acknowledges the best man's toast and toasts his bride.
- Helps his bride write personal thank-you notes for every wedding gift received before, during, and after the wedding, especially gifts received from his friends and family members.

The Supporting Cast

Every show needs a supporting cast, and, in this production, the roles are filled by the couple's parents and their attendants.

Your Parents

Traditionally, the bride's mother has the most responsibilities, although the bride's father and the groom's parents usually offer to help out any way they can. It depends a lot on how close you are to your parents and where they live. If the wedding is taking place in Chicago, it would be difficult for the parents to be intimately involved if they live in Dallas. However, even though you may be separated in a physical sense, you should honor your parents by staying in touch via e-mail or telephone so they know what's going on.

Dealing With Multiple Parents

If each of you has parents who have divorced and remarried, you could have up to eight parents and stepparents to consider in your planning. If so, I hope they're all sending money! In any case, the more parents, the more time you'll spend keeping them up to date. Also, you'll need to do some clever planning when it comes to such things as ceremony seating, which father will walk the bride down the aisle, and where to seat the various clans during the reception. Of course, if everyone gets along with each other, not to worry. If they don't, you'll need to keep them separated as much as possible during the ceremony and reception.

Mother of the Bride

The bride's mother is the most important member of the supporting cast. In fact, she's often as involved in the wedding plans as her daughter. Here are ways she can help:

- Hosts or cohosts an engagement party.
- Helps the bride shop for her gown and her attendants' attire.
- Purchases her dress first so she can let the groom's mother know what she'll be wearing to the wedding. That way the groom's mother will have an idea of the style, length, and color so she can shop for a dress that will be complementary.
- Helps compose a guest list.
- Stays in touch with the groom's parents, so they won't feel left out of the loop.
- Helps the bride and groom compile a list of choices and ideas for ceremony and reception sites, floral and decorating possibilities, caterers, pastry chef, photographer, videographer, and so forth.
- Helps address the wedding invitations.
- Helps keep track of wedding gifts.

- Helps with last-minute responsibilities, such as running crucial errands and decorating the ceremony and reception sites.
- Helps the bride get dressed on the day of the wedding.
- Stands in the receiving line, if there is one.
- Cohosts the reception with the bride's father, unless you have another couple who will be serving as host and hostess.
- During the reception, she dances with the groom.

> *If your mother is deceased, your aunt or another female relative may serve in her place.*

Father of the Bride

The bride's dad is a very important character. In fact, he's a stabilizing force as he fulfills these responsibilities:

- Hosts or cohosts an engagement party.
- Pays for all or part of the wedding expenses.
- Provides emotional support to his daughter and wife.
- Shows interest in the wedding plans, offering input on ceremony and reception sites, tuxedo styles, and ways he can help, especially as the big day draws closer.
- Runs last-minute errands, helps haul things to the church or reception, and troubleshoots problems that may pop up.
- Drives his daughter to the ceremony site, or rides in the limousine with her.

- Walks his daughter down the aisle and gives her away.
- Sits next to the bride's mother in the first pew.
- Stands in the receiving line (optional).
- Cohosts the reception with the bride's mother, unless another couple is serving as host and hostess.
- Offers a toast during the reception, usually following the toasts offered by the best man and the groom.
- During the reception, he dances with his daughter.

If your father is deceased, you may ask another male or female relative to walk you down the aisle. If your parents are divorced and have remarried, you may ask your father and stepfather to share in the duties, if appropriate. For example, your natural father may walk you down the aisle and your stepfather may be included in the ceremony in some other way, such as reading Scripture or delivering a reading. Or, your father and stepfather may both walk you down the aisle, one on each side. Another option is for your stepfather to walk you halfway, with your father escorting you the rest of the way.

Groom's Parents

The groom's parents don't play major roles in this production, but they do have several important responsibilities:

∞ Arranges a meeting with the bride's parents, preferably as soon as possible after the couple has become engaged.

∞ Hosts an engagement party (optional).

∞ The groom's father may help plan and/or attend the bachelor party.

∞ Helps pay for some of the ceremony expenses, such as designated corsages, boutonnieres, and the bride's bouquet. They may also offer to pay for some of the reception and honeymoon expenses.

∞ Helps compose a guest list.

∞ Rents or purchases their own wedding attire, after consulting with the bride, their son, and the bride's parents.

∞ Plans, cohosts, and pays for the rehearsal dinner.

∞ Escorts their son down the aisle, if it's a Jewish ceremony.

∞ The groom's mother stands in the receiving line, if there is one. The groom's father's presence in the receiving line is optional.

∞ During the reception, the groom's mother dances with her son, and the groom's father dances with the bride.

Your Attendants

Your attendants are also members of your supporting cast. They'll not only support you in the months preceding your wedding, but they'll stand beside you during the ceremony.

Your first consideration is to decide how many attendants you would like to have. Remember that the number of attendants is usually tied to the size and formality of the wedding. For example, if you'll be having a very small informal wedding with only 60 guests, you'd be top heavy with attendants if you have six bridesmaids and six groomsmen.

As you're deciding on the number of attendants, don't be caught up in trying to keep the numbers equal. Traditionally, it was imperative to have an equal number of bridesmaids and groomsmen. In today's world, however, an uneven number is fine.

Now you're ready to grab a legal pad and make a list of people who may serve as your attendants, taking into consideration important relationship problems that may pop up if you leave someone important off your list.

Here are a few factors to consider as you make your list:

Who is your closest, dearest friend?

If your closest friend is someone of the opposite sex, don't let this become a problem. It's common these days for a bride to have a *man of honor*, instead of a *maid/matron of honor*. Likewise, instead of having a *best man*, a groom may ask a woman to serve as his *best woman* or *best person*.

What about your siblings and your fiancé's siblings?

Try to include all the siblings in your wedding party, if at all possible.

It's become trendy to designate "Honorary attendants." These are attendants who are very close to you and would have been in your wedding party if they could. For example, in the case of the groom's brother who's serving in Iraq and can't come back for the wedding, he may be mentioned in the ceremony program with this suggested wording:

"Honorary best man, Jeffrey William Hastings, the groom's brother, currently serving in the U. S. Army, stationed in Iraq."

Which friends have been there for you through the years, supportive and understanding as you've faced various problems in your life?

If you find that you have 20 candidates for only six positions, you may include your extra friends in other ways. For example, you can make a big production of the candlelighting prelude by providing an abundance of candles to be lit, not only along the aisles, but on several candelabra behind the altar, and so forth. You can also include talented friends in the ceremony by having them deliver a reading, recite a poem, sing, or play a musical instrument. Other positions also need to be filled, such as reception host or hostess, and guest book and gift attendants.

It's perfectly acceptable for the groom to have two best men, such as his father and best friend. It's also proper for the bride to have two honor attendants, such as her sister as matron of honor and her best friend as maid of honor.

Which friends have asked you to serve as an attendant in their weddings?

One caveat here: you are not *obligated* to ask one of these friends to be a bridesmaid or groomsman, just because that person included you in his or her wedding. However, if he or she is on your long list anyway, you may want to promote that person to your short list.

> Don't choose your attendants based on their size, height, or attractiveness. Choose them because you love them and want them standing beside you on the most important day of your life. The bridal attendants do *not* need to be a matched set, like carriage horses.

Which people on your list would be financially able to serve as your attendants?

If someone on your list is going through a tough time financially, but you really want this person to be your attendant, offer to pick up the costs of travel and attire, discreetly, of course.

Does your ceremony venue have any religious restrictions regarding honor attendants?

If your ceremony will take place in a house of worship, check with your officiant to see if there are any religious restrictions regarding your maid/matron of honor and best man. Some faiths require that your official witnesses, aka your honor attendants, be members of that faith, and they may even be required to attend special pre-wedding classes before they'll be allowed to participate in the ceremony.

Once you've chosen the members of your wedding party, your challenge will be to let each one know as discreetly as possible what is expected.

Maid or Matron of Honor

This woman, also known as your *honor attendant* or *chief bridesmaid*, is the woman you can count on to be the most help to you during the weeks preceding the wedding, and to serve as your personal assistant during the ceremony itself. Here are her duties:

- ∞ Helps you in any way she can by addressing invitations, running errands, making telephone calls, and keeping a record of gifts received.
- ∞ Helps you shop for your bridal gown, bridal accessories, and the bridesmaids' attire.

- Serves as a sounding board as you wrestle with your wedding plans.
- Plans and hosts a bridal shower.
- Arranges a final fitting for the bridesmaids' gowns.
- Helps you pack for your honeymoon, if asked.
- Together with the bridesmaids, shops for a joint wedding gift.
- Helps you dress before the ceremony.
- Precedes you down the aisle.
- Holds your bouquet during the ceremony.
- Adjusts your veil and train after you arrive at the altar.
- Keeps the groom's ring safe until the ring ceremony.
- Signs the wedding certificate.
- Makes sure your gown and makeup look beautiful for your wedding photos.
- Stands in the receiving line, if you opt to have one.
- Dances with the best man during the reception.
- Helps you change into your going-away outfit.

> *The bride's mother may serve as her matron of honor, just as the groom's father may serve as his best man.*

Best Man

The best man is the groom's right-hand man in the days preceding the wedding and, certainly, his biggest support during the big day itself. This man should have broad shoulders, because he has the biggest load to carry:

- If the best man lives locally, he should help the groom locate an acceptable tuxedo rental store. He should also make arrangements for the groomsmen to be measured for their tuxes, and for any alterations necessary.

- Picks up the men's attire and transports it to the place where they will dress for the wedding.

- Confirms and/or picks up anything the groom has ordered, such as the bride's wedding ring that was being sized at the jewelers, or the airline tickets and travel itineraries from the travel agent.

- Plans and organizes the bachelor party.

- On the wedding day, he makes sure the groom has everything he needs for the honeymoon, including medications, passport, hotel or rental car confirmations, ATM cards, money, keys, and so forth.

- Makes last-minute telephone calls, confirming all travel and honeymoon reservations.

- He's responsible for the marriage license and sees that it is delivered to the officiant before the ceremony. He signs this document following the ceremony.

- Helps the groomsmen and ushers decorate the couple's getaway vehicle.

- Gets the groom to the ceremony on time.
- Helps the groom and the groomsmen dress.
- Keeps the bride's ring safe until the ring ceremony.
- Delivers the fee to the officiant following the ceremony.
- Helps the photographer assemble members of the wedding party or others who are to be photographed.
- Drives the bride and groom to the reception, if necessary.
- Stands in the receiving line, if there is one and he is asked.
- Dances with the bride, her mother, the maid or matron of honor, and every bridesmaid during the reception.
- Offers the first toast to the bride and groom during the reception.
- Serves as master of ceremonies for the reception, unless the bride and groom have designated an official host and hostess, or the bride's father is performing this duty.
- Helps the groom change into his going-away clothes.
- Sees that the bride's and groom's going-away luggage is placed in their getaway vehicle.
- Drives the couple to the honeymoon hotel or airport, if necessary.
- With the help of the groomsmen, the best man secures any wedding gifts that were brought to the reception.
- Returns all men's attire to the rental store.

Bridesmaids

Compared to the honor attendants, these women have very few duties:

- Help the honor attendant plan and host the bridal shower.
- Run small errands or make a few telephone calls, if asked.
- Attend the bridal luncheon.
- Stand in the receiving line, if asked.
- Smile and look pretty.

Groomsmen and Ushers

As I've already mentioned, groomsmen usually serve double duty as ushers, unless the groom has groomsmen *and* ushers, in which case their duties are different. Here are their responsibilities:

- Help the best man with pre-wedding and post-ceremony responsibilities, such as decorating the getaway vehicle and assembling the wedding party for photographs.
- If serving double duty as ushers, the groomsmen help seat the wedding guests, hand out programs, if they are provided, and roll out the aisle runner, if one is planned. The usher or groomsman offers his right arm as he escorts a woman down the aisle. If the woman is accompanied by a man, the man follows behind the woman. If a guest hands the usher or groomsman a pew card, the guest is seated according to the directions on the

card. If not, the guest is asked whether he or she is a guest of the bride or groom. The bride's guests are seated on the left and the groom's on the right for a Christian ceremony. The reverse is true for a Jewish ceremony.

- ∞ After the recessional, the groomsmen or ushers walk back down the aisle and "release" the guests by removing pew ribbons or by extending their hands toward the aisle.

- ∞ Help clean up the ceremony site before leaving for the reception, by collecting anything left behind by the guests, such as ceremony programs or personal belongings.

- ∞ One or two of the groomsmen/ushers should be available after the ceremony to give directions to the reception site, handing out pre-printed maps, if available.

- ∞ During the reception, they dance with the bride, both mothers, and every bridesmaid.

- ∞ Smile and look handsome.

If you're one of the groomsmen, pretend you're secret agents throughout the day—constantly watching for problems or potential disasters in the making. Don't get so caught up in the fun of the wedding that you forget to be on the lookout for ways you can help the best man, other members of the wedding party, guests, or service providers. Every wedding is different, so be a "007," always ready to step in and save the day.

Bit Parts

After filling the roles of your supporting cast, you're ready to audition for the bit parts, which are actually pretty important because they give the production a little color, a little spark, and a lot of charm. Several parts need to be filled, including the flower girl, ring bearer, trainbearers and pages, junior attendants, candlelighters, and bell ringers.

> *Don't include children who are too young. By "too young," one minister I spoke with said his policy is that a child must be at least 4 years old. Other wedding professionals recommend that children be no younger than 5 years old.*

Flower Girl

Your flower girl is the star of the bit parts, and she has two important responsibilities:

- ∞ Precedes the bride down the aisle, carrying a basket of flowers or tossing rose petals in the bride's path. She may walk beside the ring bearer.
- ∞ Smiles and looks adorable.

Ring Bearer

The ring bearer is another cutie and he has these responsibilities:

- ∞ Precedes the flower girl down the aisle or walks beside her. If there is no flower girl, he precedes the bride.

- ∞ Carries an elegant white or velvet pillow, or a silver tray, that has the bride's "ring" attached with a satin ribbon. Of course, this is just for show because the real ring is being safeguarded by the best man.

- ∞ If you choose to have two ring bearers, the two boys walk side by side down the aisle, and the second ring bearer carries the groom's "ring."

Trainbearers or Pages

If you have several boys and girls vying for the position of flower girl and ring bearer, and if your bridal gown happens to have a long train, extra children can serve as trainbearers or pages. This is their sole responsibility:

- ∞ Carry the train on the bridal gown during the processional and recessional.

Junior Attendants

Junior attendants are usually between 8 and 15 years of age. They don't have to work very hard. In fact, it's a matter of walking and standing:

- ∞ The bride's junior attendants are called junior bridesmaids and precede the bridesmaids down the aisle and stand next to, or at the end of, the row of bridesmaids.

- ∞ The groom's junior attendants are called junior groomsmen or ushers and stand next to, or at the end of, the row of groomsmen.

> If you're planning an encore wedding, see Chapter 17 for touching ways to involve your children in the ceremony.

Candlelighters

Candlelighters add a lot to a service, and they offer additional roles to be filled, in case you have too many girls vying for the position of junior attendant. Here are their responsibilities:

- Light the candles during the candlelighting prelude, which immediately precedes the seating of the bride's mother.
- Snuff out the candles after the recession, during the musical postlude.

Bell Ringers

Bell ringers are boys or girls of any age who walk up and down the aisles of the church or sanctuary, ringing crystal or brass bells before the ceremony begins. Traditionally, the ringing of these bells was thought to ward off any evil spirits, but in today's weddings, it's simply a way to let the guests know the ceremony is about to begin.

> Seat the parents or relatives of small children on the aisle near the front of the ceremony venue so that, if one of the cuties gets ornery or a little *too* cute up there, that person can come up to escort the child back to sit with the family.

Extras

Every big production requires extras. These roles can be filled by your friends and relatives who offer to help any way they can. Your cousin may serve as a guest book attendant, or your teenage brother as gift table attendant. A favorite aunt may offer to cut the cake during the reception, or several of your friends from your singles group may offer to help decorate the reception venue the night before the wedding.

Most of your friends and relatives will want to contribute in some way, and, believe me, you'll need their help.

Solving Puzzling People Problems

We've all heard about the squabbles that take place between cast members on the set. That's because the cast members are *people*, and wherever you find people, you'll find problems.

Here are a few typical people problems that may pop up as you're dealing with members of your wedding party, relatives, or other friends involved in your wedding.

A Friend Feels Snubbed

A relationship disaster can sneak up on you if you accidentally ask someone to be your honor attendant before you've had time to think it through. In a moment of warm, fuzzy engagement euphoria, it's easy to get carried away and ask the wrong person. For example, unless you're absolutely sure you want your sister or best friend to be your maid of honor, don't ask until you've taken time to *really* think about this important decision.

Someone Important Becomes Too Ill to Attend the Wedding

Someone who is indispensable may not be there for your big day. For example, your maid of honor may come down with the flu, or your mother may be in the hospital after emergency gallbladder surgery. So, what should you do? Usually, the best advice is to go ahead with your plans. Postponing a wedding causes monumental problems and extra expense.

If a parent is too ill to attend, ask another relative to stand in for that parent. If a member of your wedding party can't be there, you have two choices: ask another person to take that attendant's place, which is the least desirable choice, or don't worry about it. If you end up with an uneven number of bridal attendants and groomsmen, that's no big deal.

Here's a good idea—if possible, hook up a telephone line directly to the hospital room so your mom or dad can listen to the ceremony. Of course, you can also show them your wedding video when you get back from your honeymoon.

An Attendant Who Can't Afford To Be in Your Wedding

A common problem is when a member of the wedding party can't afford to rent or purchase his or her wedding attire, and either tells you so or becomes moody and broody over the expense. Although members of the wedding party are traditionally expected to pay for their own wedding attire, if you know, or even suspect, that a bridesmaid or groomsman can't afford the expense, assure that person that you'll be happy to help out with the costs. Be discreet, of course, so that there is no embarrassment.

People Who Let You Down

Another problem is when someone in your wedding party turns out to be irresponsible, aka an *airhead*. For example, your best man doesn't follow through with his duties. Even though he knows what they are, he conveniently spaces them out as he carries on with his own life and his own problems. Or, in the case of divorced parents who don't get along, the bride's father might be a no-show on her wedding day. He doesn't call—he just doesn't show! Pretty sad!

People may let you down any number of ways, so you need to face this possibility ahead of time and have a plan. Here it is: *love and tolerance*. In other words, be tolerant and loving, while quietly delegating that person's responsibilities to someone else.

In the worst case scenario, such as your dad not showing up for your wedding, have an alternate in mind—your brother, a beloved uncle, or your mother, for example. The important thing is for you to stay calm and not let these people problems throw you.

Parents Who Are Control Freaks

Here's a very common people problem: if your parents are paying for your entire wedding, they may think they have the ultimate say with the plans. They do *not*! Remember, this is *your* wedding and you're entitled to make the decisions. If you realize early on that your parents refuse to go along with this idea, you may need to plan a less expensive wedding that you can afford to pay for without their help.

An Angry Mother

Here's a biggie: As you decide which children you want to serve in your wedding, be careful not to hurt a friend's feelings by not including her child, or by including only one of her children. You haven't seen *moody* until you've seen an overly protective mother who thinks her child was spurned. The answer to this problem is to try to find some kind of job for each child. For example, if your friend's youngest daughter is serving as your flower girl, her older daughter can dress up pretty and hand out ceremony programs or stand beside the guest book attendant as her "assistant."

Chapter 5

THE
GUEST LIST

It's estimated that it takes 700 hours to plan a wedding, so it would be pretty sad if you went to all that work and didn't have an audience to watch your grand production. So, consider your guests potential members of your audience.

Compiling the guest list is one of the first, and most difficult, tasks to be completed once you become engaged. The reason it's so difficult is because, unless you have unlimited funds and can plan any size wedding, you'll need to limit the number of wedding guests to something affordable. Unfortunately, this can get real sticky because each family has certain friends and family members they feel *must* be invited to the wedding.

Another problem arises when either the bride or groom has a very large family, which makes it impossible to allot the same number of guests for each family. You'll need to do some fancy diplomacy as you juggle the allotments.

As you deal with the guest list problem, you'll probably want to follow the traditional rules of etiquette to avoid hurt feelings. Contemporary etiquette really doesn't apply to the guest list, except for a few twists which are mentioned in this chapter.

Determine the Number of Guests

Let's assume you plan to invite the same guests to the ceremony *and* the reception. This means that, although the church may hold 450 people, you may only be able to afford to feed 250 at the reception, which becomes the deciding factor. In other words, you'll need to limit your guest list to 250, even though the church actually holds more people.

If you're planning to invite a *total* of 250 guests, you'll need to take into account those spouses, significant others, and children who may accompany your guests. All those extra people can easily result in guests you hadn't planned on, so give this a lot of thought.

> Don't forget that, based on today's *average* cost of a wedding, you'll probably spend about $100 per guest. When you look at it that way, you'll no doubt compose your guest list with *great* care!

Decide How Many Guests Each Family May Invite

Traditional etiquette says that the guest list should be divided equally between the bride's and groom's families. However, in today's real world, the guest list may be split three ways, between the bride's family, the groom's family, and the couple themselves. In the case of the bride or groom who has many more family members than the other, the list may end up quite lopsided in order to be fair. The division of guests does *not* depend on how much money each family is contributing toward the wedding.

Should Invitations Be Sent to Satisfy Social or Business Obligations?

Absolutely not! A wedding is a sacred ceremony where the bride and groom should be surrounded by friends and family members with whom they have some kind of meaningful relationship. The parents, or the couple themselves, should not feel obligated to invite business acquaintances because they "owe them." This takes away from the sanctity of the ceremony, as well as the joy of being surrounded at the reception by people who mean something to you.

> Set a firm date by which you *must* receive detailed guest lists from both sets of parents, including mailing addresses and number of expected escorts or small children. If either set of parents procrastinates, this will create a lot of stress for everyone involved.

Deleting Names From an Oversized Guest List

This can become a touchy problem that requires a face-to-face meeting with both sets of parents. During this meeting you'll need to set certain parameters, such as no children, no shirttail relatives, no coworkers, and so forth. Some families decide to cut distant family members from the list. For example, if you have a great aunt you haven't seen in a dozen years, who lives a couple states away, send her a wedding announcement after the wedding, not an invitation to the wedding itself. Or, if your fiancé is an attorney for a very large law firm, he may need to limit his list to a few of his closest coworkers.

> Don't get caught up in the fallacy of thinking the more guests, the better chance you have to compensate for the cost of the wedding. First of all, you may receive *one* gift for every two to four guests, especially when you realize that a couple or a family often goes together to purchase it. Certainly, you can't count on cash gifts covering your expenses. It just won't happen.

Should Children Be Invited?

This is a crucial question, unless you'll have plenty of room and food at your reception. Depending on the number of children, you'll undoubtedly need to provide babysitters and a playroom for the children during the reception. Special children's buffet tables have also become trendy, providing child-friendly foods that are less expensive than the rest of your reception fare.

> You may decide to limit your guest list to children who are at least 16 or 18 years of age. If you hold to this rule, there shouldn't be hard feelings. However, don't be surprised if a few guests show up with their younger children anyway. Sorry about that!

Should Spouses Always Be Invited?

Yes, spouses should always be invited, even though you may not know them personally. It's considered very poor taste to invite a guest, but exclude the spouse. You should also invite significant others and fiancés.

May Single Guests Bring a Date?

This is one of the biggest questions you'll need to answer as you compose your guest list. If many of your friends are singles who may feel uncomfortable attending a wedding and dance reception without a date, you may decide to allow for dates. However, if you plan to spend a set amount of money on your reception food and drink, you may need to limit the number of escorts invited. Otherwise, if you want everyone to feel comfortable at your wedding, you might opt for less expensive reception food, such as a champagne and hors d'oeuvres reception, or a light brunch buffet following a mid-morning wedding.

Are We Required to Invite Everyone Who Was Invited to a Pre-Wedding Party?

Yes, except in certain circumstances. For example, your coworkers may throw you a little lunchtime bridal shower, although they know you're planning a small wedding limited to family and very close personal friends. Otherwise, it's in poor taste to exclude someone from the wedding guest list who was invited to an engagement party or a wedding shower.

Can We Have Separate Guest Lists for the Ceremony and for the Reception?

Absolutely! The ceremony-only guest list is composed of those who are not invited to your reception. The ceremony/reception guest list would be sent invitations to the ceremony, but with separate enclosure cards inviting them to a reception at another venue.

> Separate guest lists are popular these days. *Personally*, I don't like them because you're taking a chance that you might hurt feelings. What if a ceremony guest who *has* been invited to the reception accidentally says to an *uninvited* guest, "See you at the reception!" How do you think that will make the uninvited guest feel? My personal preference is to invite *all* the ceremony guests to the reception, even if it means serving less expensive food.

How Do We Handle Relationship Problems Between Family Members?

Divorced parents who don't get along can cause sparks at a wedding, unless they are handled with kid gloves. Likewise, grown siblings who aren't speaking to each other, or anyone else who threatens not to come to the wedding if the "enemy" will be there can leave you stuck in the middle. What do you do?

Here's the answer: this is *your* wedding. Invite the people you love and really want to be present on your wedding day. Then, once you've made that decision, all you can do is try to keep the feuding family members apart by seating them a couple rows apart during the ceremony and at different tables during the reception.

If someone threatens to boycott your wedding if you invite someone else, go ahead and invite them both anyway, and if one of them doesn't show up, it's not your problem. On the other hand, if your parents are divorced and your dad refuses to walk you down the aisle if your mom is there with her new squeeze, you *do* have a big problem! If anyone drops to this level of immaturity, you'll need to let it roll off your back and, in the case of a surly dad, ask your brother or someone else to walk you down the aisle.

The important thing for you to remember is that this is your party and if a guest, even one of your parents, acts like a selfish, immature brat, don't let it ruin your day.

> *If a problem or confrontation evolves during the ceremony or reception, have someone designated ahead of time to gently escort the offending parties off the premises.*

What About Creating an Alternate Guest List, in Case Many Guests on the First-String List Decline?

Personally, I don't approve of alternate guest lists, not only because they're in poor taste, but they're potential time bombs! The reason why these lists are popular these days is because they give the families a list to fall back on if the first-stringers can't make it to the wedding. However, this is risky business that can cause hurt feelings if a second-stringer finds out he wasn't invited first. If you decide to have an alternate guest list, the only guests who should be placed on it are faraway friends or relatives who don't know any of the first-stringers. Otherwise, when they *are* invited, they'll realize they were backup guests.

Finally, if you do opt for an alternate list, don't mail invitations to anyone on this list if it's closer than one month before the wedding.

> *Don't make handwritten guest lists, because this can cause misspellings when addressing the invitations, especially if someone else will be helping with this chore. Instead, create your guest lists on your computer.*

Chapter 6

PRE-WEDDING FESTIVITIES

Once you become engaged, the fun begins! You and your fiancé will be honored guests at several affairs between now and the wedding, so sit back, relax, and bask in your 15 minutes of fame, as you look forward to your co-starring roles in the upcoming production!

The rules of traditional etiquette have been relaxed considerably when it comes to these parties and celebrations, although certain rules still apply, as you'll see.

Bridal Showers

A bridal shower isn't *mandatory*, although one of these parties is usually hosted by the maid or matron of honor, with the bridesmaids' help. Although traditional etiquette says that it's in very poor taste for a family member to host one of these showers, it's become acceptable for the bride's sister to host or cohost a bridal shower, if she happens to be one of the bridesmaids. The mother of the bride, her grandmother, or an aunt usually do not host a bridal shower, *unless* this is common practice in the family's ethnic or cultural background. In most cultures, however, this is considered a blatant request for gifts.

Although a bridal shower may be a quite proper, formal bridal tea, it's usually a more informal affair. It may be a buffet or sit-down luncheon in a private home, or as casual as a patio barbecue or getting together over lunch at a restaurant. The bride may be honored with several of these lovely affairs.

It's preferable for a bridal shower to be held at least two weeks before the wedding, because there are too many other things going on close to the wedding date. The exception would be when one or more of the bridesmaids lives out of town and can't host a party until she arrives a few days before the wedding.

If the bride's honor attendant is a man, aka *man of honor*, he may plan a co-ed or couples' party instead of a bridal shower, with the help of the best man and all the bridesmaids and groomsmen.

Bridal Shower Trends and Traditions

- ∞ Don't invite anyone to a bridal shower who won't also be invited to the wedding, except in certain cases, such as a group of coworkers or club members who don't necessarily expect to be invited to the wedding.

- ∞ Other than members of the wedding party, the same guests should not be invited to multiple parties. If a guest *is* invited to more than one party, that guest should not feel obligated to bring more than one gift.

- ∞ The gifts' ribbons are usually fashioned into a *pretend bridal bouquet*, which the bride carries during the wedding rehearsal. This fake bouquet is constructed by making small slits in a sturdy paper plate, through which the ribbons are pulled, with several longer ribbons dangling down.

∞ One of the bridesmaids surreptitiously records exactly what the bride says as she opens each gift, then reads her statements out loud after all the gifts have been opened. According to light-hearted tradition, her remarks are supposed to be what she will say on her wedding night.

∞ If the party is a formal bridal tea, proper etiquette dictates that the bride's maid or matron of honor must be the one who pours the tea.

Co-Ed Showers

A co-ed shower, aka couples' shower, is a fun party attended by the bride and groom, their attendants, and their male and female friends. This type of party is usually more active than a bridal shower, where the women typically sit most of the time. A successful co-ed party is one where the guests get involved, plus the refreshments are heartier because hungry men are present. Real men *may* eat quiche, but they consider finger sandwiches as mere appetizers, so serve something everyone will enjoy, such as pizza or barbecued steaks.

For wedding shower ideas, see my book, *Complete Book of Wedding Showers* (Career Press, 1997).

Bridal Luncheon

The bridal luncheon, also called the bridesmaids' luncheon, differs from the typical bridal shower in several ways:

- The guests are a select group, usually composed of the bride and her attendants, although in certain parts of the country and within certain ethnic groups, it's considered proper etiquette to invite the mothers of the bride and groom, the mothers of the flower girl and the ring bearer, plus the couple's sisters.

- This luncheon may be held closer to the wedding date than a bridal shower, usually two days or so before the wedding, especially if the bride's attendants must travel to the wedding from out of the area.

- This luncheon is usually hosted by the maid or matron of honor, with help from the bridesmaids, but it may be hosted by the bride herself.

- The luncheon usually takes place in an upscale restaurant or tearoom, or in a private home.

- Gifts are traditionally exchanged during this little party: the bridesmaids present the bride with a joint gift, usually something special for the bride to wear on her wedding day. The bride also presents her attendants with individual gifts, usually a piece of jewelry to be worn during the wedding, such as matching pearl necklaces.

- The expense of this luncheon is paid by the bridesmaids, if they are hosting it, or the bride picks up the tab if she is the hostess.

∞ A sweet, sentimental tradition during this party is to serve a pink cake with small charms hidden between the layers, each attached to a ribbon. Each charm has a special meaning for the woman who pulls it from the cake. For example, a horseshoe or four-leaf clover means you'll experience good luck; a heart means love will come to you soon; and an anchor means exciting travels are ahead. Each single woman pulls a ribbon. The one who pulls out the wedding ring charm is said to be the next to wed.

Bachelorette Party

The traditionally rowdy bachelorette party, with male strippers or an X-rated movie, has given way to a day at the spa; lunch and a shopping spree; an evening at a live musical or theatrical performance; or a day on the ski slopes. It's considered more of a fun escape than an actual party, usually several hours spent together doing something special. It's often scheduled to coincide with the groom's bachelor party.

Bachelor Party

Traditionally, the bachelor party has been considered a "last night out with the boys," complete with a keg of beer and a stripper who pops out of a cake. Times have changed, however, and according to my research and that of other journalists who have interviewed today's grooms, the trend is more towards sports-oriented get-togethers, casino weekends, poker parties, or good old-fashioned roasts.

It's a fun time when all the men involved can get together before the wedding, including the groom's close friends, the members of his wedding party, his father, and his brothers.

The party may be hosted by the groom, the best man or best woman, the groom's father, or as a joint effort by all the groom's buddies. Traditionally, it's been held the night before the wedding, but it makes more sense to have it a week or so before, for obvious reasons. Not only is the evening before the wedding usually reserved for the rehearsal and rehearsal dinner, but it's also a good idea to avoid a hangover on the big day.

> Gifts are often exchanged during one of these get-togethers. The groom usually gives individual gifts to each of the men in his wedding party, and the men often go together on a joint gift for the groom.

Whatever type of bachelor party is planned, it's nice to include a traditional toast by the groom to his bride (even though she isn't present). He should stand, raise his glass and simply say, "To my bride," which will be followed by all the men who stand and join him in the toast.

Pre-Wedding Breakfast or Lunch

If the wedding is scheduled for late afternoon or evening, it's nice if someone hosts a light breakfast or luncheon for the couple's parents and members of the wedding party. Ideally, it should be hosted by someone who isn't directly involved in the wedding, such as a neighbor, an aunt, or a close friend of the bride's or groom's parents. This little meal should be light and easy. It may take place at the ceremony venue, especially if it only involves finger foods, such as breakfast rolls, fruit, sandwiches, or cookies. The bride and groom may or may not attend, especially if they want to avoid seeing each other before the ceremony.

Party Invitations

Party invitation etiquette varies depending on the party's formality. However, most invitations should include the following:

- ∞ Name(s) of the guest(s) of honor.
- ∞ Name(s) of the host(s).
- ∞ Date and time.
- ∞ Location of the party, with map or directions included, if necessary. Also, include the telephone number for the party site, in case anyone gets lost.
- ∞ The party's theme and dress code, if applicable.
- ∞ Suggested gift ideas or a list of gift registries, plus color preferences and sizes, if applicable.
- ∞ R.S.V.P. information (be sure to include a deadline).

Formal invitations should be mailed four weeks ahead of time. Informal invitations may be mailed two to three weeks before the party.

Example of a formal invitation:

You are invited to attend a formal bridal tea
in honour of
Miss Jennifer Elise Tobin
hosted by the Misses Ashley Jameson and Elizabeth Torrey
Saturday, June twentieth at one o'clock
1550 Santa Maria Circle

Please R.S.V.P. by June 15   *Bridal Registry*
555-1728   *Camela's Bridal Treasures*

Example of an informal invitation:

Come to a Luau
honoring our favorite couple
the Big Kauna (Jeff) and his sweet Wahini (Darcy)!
Wear your Hawaiian shirts or muumuus.
2020 Mendocino Lane
April 10th
7 p.m.
R.S.V.P. Joni or Jim by April 5th
555-8881

Although proper etiquette dictates that the bride and groom should write thank-you notes to each person who hosts a party and to everyone who brings a gift, that rule has been softened somewhat in today's society. Today the only thank-you note that is actually required is to the party hosts and to anyone who sent a gift to the party, but was unable to attend. Everyone else can be thanked during the party.

Chapter 7

THE WEDDING COSTUMES

A wedding resembles a theatrical production, which means that it needs costumes. Your choice of wedding attire will be determined by the formality, style, and theme of your wedding.

How formal will your wedding be? And will your wedding have a certain style or theme? For example, are you planning a Renaissance wedding or a country-western wedding? Or, will your wedding be inspired by your family's ethnicity? If so, many of the suggestions given in this chapter will need to be modified to accommodate themed or ethnic costumes.

Here are the traditional and contemporary rules of etiquette regarding wedding attire, depending on the formality of the wedding.

Bride

The bride's gown is the most important wedding costume. In fact, her gown should be purchased first, before any other wedding attire has been rented or purchased. Here are general guidelines for the bridal gown for each degree of formality:

Ultraformal Evening Wedding

- Floor-length gown with embellishments, such as beading, embroidery, or lace overlay.
- The gown may have long or short sleeves, however, if short sleeved, the bride should wear elbow-length gloves.
- Her gown's train and veil should be floor length or longer.

Ultraformal Daytime Wedding

- Floor-length gown, but less elaborate than for an evening wedding.
- The gown may have long or short sleeves; however, if short sleeved, the bride should wear elbow-length gloves.
- The gown's train and veil may be shorter than it would be for an evening wedding.

> During the ring vows, the bride's glove on her left hand may be removed for the placement of the ring, or the ring finger on the glove may be cut so that it can be easily removed during the ring ceremony. A third option, and this is my favorite, is to wear fingerless gloves.

Formal Evening Wedding

- Cathedral- or chapel-length gown.
- Chapel- or sweep-length train and veil.
- If the gown is short sleeved, the bride should wear elbow-length gloves.

Formal Daytime Wedding

- The same cathedral- or chapel-length gown as required for a formal evening wedding.
- Chapel- or sweep-length train and veil or an elaborate ankle-length gown with a shorter veil.
- If the gown has a floor-length train, it may be detachable.

Semiformal Evening Wedding

- Floor-length gown with no train.

or

- An ankle-length gown in white, ivory, or pastel.
- Veil is elbow-length or shorter

Semiformal Daytime Wedding

- Same requirements as a semiformal evening wedding, except that the veil should be shorter.
- A bridal headpiece with a blusher veil is acceptable.

Informal Daytime or Evening Wedding

- Cocktail length dress.

or

- A suit or street length dress.
- Usually, no veil, although the cocktail dress allows for a short blusher veil attached to flowers or a simple headband.
- In lieu of a veil, she may wear a hat or flowers in her hair.

> Some religions require that the bride wear a face veil, so if you plan to be married in a place of worship, ask the officiant before purchasing your veil or choosing an alternative headpiece.

Casual Wedding

∽ Depending on the wedding's theme, the bride may wear anything she likes. For example, she might wear jeans, boots, and a western shirt for a country-western wedding, or a sarong and sandals for a Polynesian wedding.

Groom

Before the groom decides on attire for himself and his attendants, he, his bride, and their wedding coordinator should visit a formalwear store for a consultation. Once the store's consultant gathers all the facts, he'll be able to present various options, depending on the style and formality of your wedding.

Here is suggested attire for each degree of formality:

Ultraformal Evening Wedding

∽ Tailcoats with matching trousers.

∽ Wing-collared shirt with white bow tie.

∽ White waistcoat.

∽ White gloves and black top hat are optional.

Ultraformal Daytime Wedding

- ∞ Cutaway coat with grey striped trousers.
- ∞ Wing-collared shirt with ascot or striped tie.
- ∞ Grey waistcoat.
- ∞ Grey gloves and black top hat are optional.

Formal Evening Wedding

- ∞ Tuxedo or white dinner jacket and complementary trousers, depending on the season.
- ∞ Dress shirt and bow tie.
- ∞ Vest or cummerbund.

Formal Daytime Wedding

- ∞ Grey stroller with striped trousers.
- ∞ Wing-collared shirt with striped tie.

or

- ∞ For summer, a white suit with dress shirt, bow tie, vest, or cummerbund.

Semiformal or Informal Evening Wedding

- ∞ Dark suit with white or colored shirt and four-in-hand tie.

or

- ∞ Dinner jacket and matching trousers, with dress shirt, bow tie, vest, or cummerbund.

or

- ∞ Navy blazer with white or grey slacks, depending on the season, with dress shirt and four-in-hand tie.

> The men's formalwear market has become so sophisticated that there are dozens of styles to consider. Before making your choice, pick up a brochure from your local formalwear rental store to bring home and consider at your leisure. Or, you can view many styles over the Internet with a click of your mouse. For example, take a look at *davidsformalwear.com* and *afterhours.com*. The After Hours formalwear Website features color photos of real men modeling 56 different styles of tuxes and suits, and the David's Formalwear Website also offers "gently used tuxedo packages" that are for sale.

Casual Wedding

Wear something that complements your bride's attire, depending on where your wedding takes place. That is, unless, you're like the couple a wedding planner told me about who arrived stark naked riding double on a motorcycle. They were married beside a mountain stream, surrounded by the rest of the members of their motorcycle club. Now—that's what I call a *casual* wedding!

Members of Your Wedding Party

Each person in your wedding party is a cast member in this impressive production, aka your wedding. And as cast members, they need costumes that are complementary to the theme and formality of your ceremony.

Bridesmaids

The bridesmaids' gowns should complement the bride's gown in formality, with this one caveat: they should never be longer or more elaborate than the bridal gown.

Although etiquette doesn't demand it, the maid or matron of honor's gown is usually slightly different and more elaborate than the bridesmaids' gowns. Her attire should stand out so the guests will recognize her as the honor attendant. If the bride's honor attendant is a man, his attire should be the same as the best man.

As the bride considers various gowns for her attendants, she should be sensitive to the differences in her bridesmaids' figures. A gown won't necessarily flatter everyone. I know of a wedding where the bride had her heart set on strapless floor-length gowns for her attendants. This was fine except for one of the bridesmaids who was so well endowed that she was almost falling out of the dress. She begged the bride to make another choice, but the bride was adamant—she wanted the strapless dresses. The full-busted bridesmaid went along with it just to please her friend, but she was uncomfortable and embarrassed all day long. Don't do this to your bridesmaids. Choose something that flatters each of your attendants, even if you must select a different style gown for each attendant in the same or a similar fabric. Companies such as David's Bridal offer mix and match two piece dresses in a variety of styles and colors.

I can't count the times I'm asked about tattoos. For example, in the case of a bridesmaid who has a tattoo on her shoulder, should the bride choose bridesmaids' gowns with sleeves, so the tattoo won't show? It all depends on the tattoo. If the tattoo is a beautiful little butterfly, it's quite acceptable for it to show. However, in the case of a less tasteful tattoo, the bride can decide whether she wants it covered or not.

Junior Bridesmaids

The junior bridesmaids' dresses may be more youthful versions of the bridesmaids' gowns, if the wedding is ultraformal, formal, or semiformal. For an informal wedding, a junior attendant may wear a nice dress in any color complementary to those worn by the bridesmaids. Designers such as Jim Helm offer junior bridesmaids dresses that are smaller, more age appropriate versions of their bridesmaids dresses.

Flower Girl and Trainbearer

For an ultraformal, formal, or semiformal wedding, the flower girl or trainbearer may wear a white organza pinafore over a pastel, print, or velvet dress, with opaque or lace tights and patent leather shoes or ballet slippers. Or, she may wear a custom-designed copy of the bride's or bridesmaids' gown, made from the same or similar fabric. For an informal wedding, she may wear an existing dress in white, or any color that complements the bridesmaids' gowns. These dresses may be personalized for the wedding by adding wide sashes in the same color as the bridesmaids' gowns.

> The attire for a flower girl and a ring bearer should complement each other; likewise, if you choose to have one trainbearer (girl) and one page (boy) carrying your train, be sure their ensembles complement each other as well.

Candlelighters

Candlelighters may be boys or girls. If yours are girls, they may wear dresses similar, but not necessarily identical, to those worn by the bridesmaids or junior bridesmaids.

Likewise, boys may wear outfits similar to the groomsmen (ushers) or the junior groomsmen.

Groomsmen or Ushers

The best man's attire is usually the same as the groom's, which distinguishes him from the groomsmen, whose attire may be slightly less elaborate. For example, the groom and best man may wear vests that differ from the groomsmen. The most important thing is for the men to have a uniform appearance with consistent tailoring. Here are guidelines:

- The tuxedo jackets should fit snugly, but with no arm bulges, plus there should be a little room at the waist.

- Sleeves should end at the men's wrist bones.

- Trousers should touch the top of the shoes with enough slack so the crease breaks slightly.

- The shirt collars should be tight enough to hug the neck, but not so tight that the lapels buckle. Ask your rental store for a supply of collar extenders—they're great to have on hand at the last minute.

- If the groom has a best woman instead of best man, she should wear a gown that is similar to the bridesmaids' gowns. She doesn't carry a bouquet, however, but wears a corsage instead.

It's become popular for the groom and his groomsmen to purchase their tuxedos, instead of renting them. That way, for only a little more money than a rental fee, the men have tuxedos in their closets for future events.

Ring Bearer or Page

If a ring bearer or page is 6 years old or younger, he may wear shorts, jacket, dress shirt, and bow tie. If he is older than 6 years of age, he may wear a younger version of the groomsmen's attire or a dark blue Eton suit or, because companies such as Ralph Lauren offer child sizes, a tuxedo. For an informal wedding, he may wear any nice existing outfit.

Junior Groomsman or Usher

This boy may wear a younger version of the groomsmen's or usher's attire.

Parents

The parents should choose attire that's not only appropriate to the wedding's formality, but also complementary to the bride's gown and the attendants' attire.

Bride's and Groom's Mothers

- ∞ The mothers' gowns or dresses should never be more formal than the bride's gown. If the bride's gown is floor length, the mothers' dresses may also be floor length or street length; however, if the bride's gown is not floor length, the mothers' dresses should be no longer than the bride's gown.
- ∞ The mothers' gowns should be complementary to those worn by the bridesmaids. The two gowns shouldn't be the same, however. Each should have its own style. An elegant suit is always a nice choice and a hat is optional for an ultraformal or formal wedding.

∞ The bride's mother is obligated to choose her dress or gown first, then furnish the groom's mother with a photo or drawing so she may select attire that is complementary in style and color. The bride's mother should take care of this responsibility as soon as she possibly can, so the groom's mom has plenty of time to shop.

∞ It's in poor taste for either mother to wear anything sexy or provocative. For example, don't wear a miniskirt or a dress that is low-cut or backless. I attended a wedding where the bride wore a formal, white, floor-length gown, but her mother, who has a fantastic figure and was at one time a professional figure skating diva, wore a short, sexy, see-through costume with dangling, shimmering fringe. I felt sorry for the bride.

∞ It's also considered poor taste for the mothers to wear white, because their dresses will compete with the bride's gown.

Just a word about women wearing black. Although black gowns have become quite popular for brides-maids' attire, especially for a Black and White Wedding where everyone wears either black or white, it's actually considered by some to be in poor taste. This is because, tra-ditionally in many cultures, black has been associated with death and mourning.

Bride's and Groom's Fathers

∞ The bride's father should follow the lead set by the groomsmen, wearing the same or similar attire.

∞ The groom's father may do likewise, or he
may wear a nice dark suit.

Helpers

The helpers and volunteers should be furnished with
a photo or color sample of the attire being worn by the
members of the wedding party. That way they can wear
something similar in style and formality and in a complementary color.

Chapter 8

WEDDING INVITATIONS, ANNOUNCEMENTS, AND SUCH

Your wedding stationery will set the tone for your wedding, from the invitations, which are the first things your guests will see, to the enclosure cards, thank-you notes, wedding announcements, and any other wedding-related items you may decide to order. For example, you may order printed cocktail napkins, matches, place cards, and other wedding memorabilia.

Although today's contemporary wedding stationery is more creative and personal than the traditional stationery of the past, certain rules of traditional etiquette still apply as you make your selections. The more formal the wedding, the closer these rules should be followed.

Once you've chosen a theme for your wedding and decided on its formality, you're ready to go shopping. Remember that the quality and texture of the paper, the color and style of the lettering, the way the invitation is worded, and the manner in which your envelopes are addressed should all be in keeping with your wedding's theme and formality, as well as your own personality.

Wedding Invitations and Enclosures

Your wedding invitations could be considered playbills or press releases for your theatrical production. Order your invitations and enclosures at least four months in advance, preferably six months. This will not only give you time to catch any typos, but will allow time to address and assemble the invitations at a leisurely pace. If you plan to hire a professional calligrapher to address your envelopes, I recommend ordering your invitations eight months in advance. Or, ask to have the envelopes shipped immediately so that the calligrapher can get started before the rest of the order arrives.

If your wedding will be ultraformal or formal, your invitations and enclosures should be engraved, which is a raised print that is pressed through and can be felt on the back of the paper. The engraving should be with black ink, using the Roman font style.

Less formal printing techniques are thermography, which results in a raised print that is shinier than engraving; lithography, which imprints the lettering with ink, but does not result in raised letters; and laser printing, using a computer.

Invitations for a casual wedding may be extended any way you like: with a telephone call, in person, via e-mail, or with handwritten notes.

If you prefer professionally printed invitations, you'll see examples of the various printing techniques when you visit your stationer, along with dozens of sample phrasings.

Sample Wordings for Wedding Invitations

The names at the top of the invitations are traditionally considered to be the hosts of the wedding, although contemporary etiquette doesn't hold to this rule.

Traditional Ultraformal or Formal Wedding

Mr. and Mrs. Howard James Michaels
request the honour of your presence
at the marriage of their daughter
Katrina Anne

to

Mr. Todd Edward Benton
Saturday, the fifth of June
Two thousand five
at two o'clock
Maplewood Community Church
Maplewood, New York

Exceptions

∽ For a civil ceremony, or a less formal ceremony, use the wording "the pleasure of your company" in place of "the honour of your presence."

∽ If you and your fiancé are sending your own invitations, and no parents are involved, change the previously recommended wording of the invitation to read:

The honour of your presence
is requested at the marriage of
Miss Ashley Leanne Sylva

to

Mr. Phillip James Dotson
(and so on)

∽ If one of your parents has passed away, replace "Mr. and Mrs. James Howard Brandon" with "Mrs. James Howard Brandon" or "Mr. James Howard Brandon." (If your mother is the survivor, a formal invitation must use her husband's name, but for an informal invitation, she may use *"Mrs. Helen Brandon"* instead.)

∞ If your mother was widowed, has remarried, and she and your stepfather are hosting the wedding, use this wording to avoid confusion:

> *Mr. and Mrs. Edward James Harris*
> *request the honour of your presence*
> *at the marriage of her daughter*
> *Miss Sheryl Annette Smythe*
> *(and so on)*

∞ If your parents divorced, have both remarried, and both couples want to host your wedding, simply include the names of both couples at the top of the invitation:

> *Mr. and Mrs. Andrew James Kata*
> *and*
> *Mr. and Mrs. John Robert Cain*
> *(and so on)*

∞ If the bride's parents are deceased and the groom's parents are hosting the wedding, use this wording: (Note that, in this case, the bride's name is preceded by "Miss" and the "Mr." is dropped from the groom's name.)

> *Mr. and Mrs. Carter Ronald Hilton*
> *request the honour of your presence*
> *at the marriage of*
> *Miss Denise Anne Anderson*
> *to their son*
> *Gordon John Hilton*
> *(and so on)*

☙ If a relative is hosting the wedding for any reason, but especially if both parents are deceased:

> *Mr. and Mrs. John Eugene Martin*
> *request the honour of your presence*
> *at the marriage of their granddaughter*
> *Lisa Marie Kennedy*
> *(and so on)*

☙ If your wedding is being cohosted by your children, see chapter 17 (Encore Wedding) for sample wordings.

☙ If it is a military wedding, rank determines how an invitation is worded. Unless the bride's or groom's rank is sergeant or higher, the rank is omitted entirely, with only the mention of the branch of service. If either is a junior officer, the bride's or groom's rank is given on the line below the name. If higher than lieutenant, the title is placed in front of the name.

Examples:

Below sergeant:	John Ellis MacCrae United States Army
Junior officer:	John Ellis MacCrae First Lieutenant, United States Navy
Higher than Lt.:	Captain John Ellis MacCrae, United States Navy

Informal Wedding

Two lives, two hearts
joined together in friendship
united forever in love.
It is with joy that we,
Judith Anne Larson
and
Jason Randolph Gray
invite you to share
in a celebration of love
as we exchange our marriage vows
on Saturday, the twentieth of January
at one-thirty in the afternoon
in the garden of
2231 Cedar Avenue
Dallas, Texas

Enclosure Cards and Sample Wordings

It should be noted that sending a response card is considered poor taste because, according to traditional etiquette, guests have always been expected to reply with a handwritten note, either accepting or declining the invitation. However, because we live in a harried, hectic world, invited guests have stopped abiding by this rule of etiquette. Hence, the necessity for response cards.

Response Cards

(aka R.S.V.P. cards, which is French for *repondez s'il vous plait,* which means "please respond.")

Kindly respond by August second

M _____

_____ persons will attend

or

Name: _____

Accepts with pleasure: _____

Declines with regrets: _____

Some brides use pencil to lightly number the backs of response cards, with the numbers corresponding to their master list of invitations. That way, if a response card is returned with the name missing, she can match it up with the number on the master list.

Within the Ribbon Cards

This is a simple card that has the words "within the ribbon" printed in the center. Any guest receiving this enclosure card should sit in one of the pews designated for them, usually decorated in a special way with ribbons or flowers. The ushers should be alerted that anyone handing them a card with these words should be escorted to these designated pews.

At Home Cards

An at home card gives the bride's new address after she is married.

Rain Cards

A rain card gives the alternate locations for the wedding and/or reception in case of rain.

Admission Cards

Admission cards are only needed if the ceremony is being held in a venue that attracts sightseers. The guest is to present the admission card at the entrance to the facility. The card may say, "*Please present this card at St. John's Cathedral for admittance.*"

Map Cards

A map card is a small card that gives directions and/or a map to the ceremony and/or reception sites.

Parking Cards

Wedding guests should *never* be expected to pay for parking when attending your ceremony and/or reception. Make arrangements with the parking garages near your venues to pick up the tab for any guest parking fees (furnish the attendant with a copy of the parking card for identification). This requires parking card enclosures in the invitation, which the guest presents to the parking attendant when exiting the garage. Sample wording:

For free parking, present this card to the attendant
when you exit the Collierville parking garage,
located at 2110 Collierville Avenue

Reception Cards

Dinner Reception
to be held following ceremony
in the Rose Garden Room
Hilton Hotel
881 North Prince Avenue

or

Luncheon Reception
immediately following ceremony
in Augusta Annex

or

Cocktail Reception
immediately following ceremony
Riverside View Restaurant
Number 1 River Road

In lieu of separate reception cards, the reception information may be added in small lettering on a lower corner of the invitation.

Assembling and Addressing Wedding Invitations

- Enclose any enclosure cards inside the invitation.
- Enclose the invitation inside the inner envelope, which may be addressed as follows:

Mr. and Mrs. Henry Smith

or

Miss (or Ms.) Stewart and Mr. Howard

or

Mr. and Mrs. Henry Smith, Jeremy and Sarah

- ∽ The front of the inner envelope should face the *back* of the outer envelope.
- ∽ Address the outer envelope with the guests' full names, such as:

Mr. and Mrs. Henry James Smith
551 North Oleander Way
Tucson, Arizona 85737

or

Miss Leanna Estello Stewart
2202 Elm Way, etc.

- ∽ Initials are never used, if you don't know the full name:

Mr. and Mrs. Henry James Smith

not

Mr. and Mrs. Henry J. Smith

- ∽ Cities, states, and numbered streets are always written out in full:

2004 Eighth Boulevard
Madison, Arizona 85781

- ∽ When addressing an invitation to an unmarried couple at the same address, the names should be written on separate lines in alphabetical order:

Miss (Ms.) Janice Jameson
Mr. Boyd Randolph

∞ When addressing an invitation to a widowed woman, use her married name:

Mrs. David Bandon

If your wedding is to be a formal black-tie affair, it's proper etiquette to let your guests know so they can dress appropriately. Add the words "Black Tie Invited" in small letters at the bottom of your invitations.

Helpful Tips

∞ Order 25 extra invitations, just in case you decide to invite more guests than you originally planned. Also, order extra envelopes, just in case you make a mistake when addressing an invitation. It's much less expensive to order extras up front than to go back and reorder at a later date.

∞ If you're not inviting children to your wedding, the parents should get the message when they see that their children's names are not included on the invitation. Unfortunately, it's considered very poor etiquette to print "No Children" on the invitation. If you're afraid the parents will bring their children anyway—and many will—ask friends and family members to tactfully spread the word that due to space and costs, children will not be able to attend.

- Always address your invitations by hand, using blue or black ink, and be sure both envelopes (outer and inner) are in the same handwriting.

- Always add postage to the response cards; otherwise, invited guests may not go to the trouble to mail them back to you.

- An invitation to a married guest always includes the spouse.

- Everyone who participates in the wedding should be mailed wedding invitations, including the officiant and his or her spouse.

- For a formal wedding, mail your invitations six to eight weeks in advance; for an informal wedding, mail them four weeks in advance. If enclosing response cards, request they be returned no later than three weeks before the wedding. Traditionally, the invitations should be mailed from the hometown of the bride's parents, although this rule isn't always followed, which is fine. Another rule of etiquette—and this rule *does* still hold today— is that the envelopes should never be run through a postal machine. Each envelope should have a postage stamp, just like an ordinary letter.

- It's never acceptable, under any circumstances, to list the names of the stores where you have established gift registries at the bottom of the invitation, or as an insert. It's also considered poor etiquette to add the words: "No gifts, please."

- State on the invitation what the guests can expect in the way of food to be served at the reception. This will give them an idea how much to eat before the wedding, saving room for the "feast," or filling up before the "famine." Simply state, in small italicized lettering at the bottom of the invitation "Dinner reception to follow" or "Hors d'oeuvres reception to follow," for example.

∞ Never, *ever* print "BYOB" at the bottom of a wedding or reception invitation, no matter how informal it is.

∞ When addressing your invitations, do not seal the invitation and then address the outer envelope. The pressure of the pen can leave an imprint on the inner envelope and/or the ink may bleed through and stain it.

∞ Never use stick-on return address labels.

∞ The invitations and all the enclosure cards should have the same style font.

∞ The invitations' return address should be the address where replies are sent and gifts are delivered before the wedding, preferably a street address (not a post office box).

∞ It's considered poor etiquette to address an invitation to someone "and guest" or "and family." If you invite a single woman, for example, and want to include her steady boyfriend, call her to get his name so that it can be included, written out in full, on the outer and inner envelope.

∞ Inner envelopes are addressed in dark blue or black ink with the titles and last names, or using their first and last names. Example: *Mr. and Mrs. Parsons* or *George and Judy Parsons*

∞ It's no longer necessary to include tissue inserts. This old tradition was a necessity in the days when the ink smeared.

- Outer envelopes are addressed with all streets, cities, and states written out entirely with no abbreviations allowed. Example: *1881 East Pennsylvania Boulevard; Hazelwood, Washington.*

- To assemble the invitation, insert the enclosure cards; place each invitation face up inside the inner envelope; insert the inner envelope inside the outer envelope, with the written name on the inner envelope facing the back of the outer envelope; seal the outer envelope; and weigh for proper postage before mailing.

- Announcements are never sent to anyone who has been invited to the ceremony or reception; they are mailed two days after the wedding.

- Keep track of your R.S.V.P.s by creating a Master List (preferably on your computer) with these headings:

  Date invitation sent:

  Name and address of guest:

  Response (Yes, No, How many?):

  Gift received:

  Thank-you note sent?

- Mail all the invitations at once on the same day. Do not mail them as they are addressed.

An R.S.V.P. is usually not included on an invitation to the ceremony only. The purpose of the R.S.V.P. is to find out how many guests are coming to your reception.

By adding gift information to your Master List, you'll not only have everything together, but you'll have each guest's address handy for writing those thank-you notes.

By the way, if you haven't received an R.S.V.P. within two weeks of the wedding, delegate someone to call the guest(s).

> *Even though it may seem more convenient to hand-deliver invitations, especially to neighbors, close friends, or coworkers, wedding invitations should always be mailed directly to the homes of the invited guests.*

Save-the-Date Cards

These one-sided cards are often sent a year or more in advance to revered family members and close friends who won't want to miss the wedding by planning a cruise or some other activity on your wedding day. If you're getting married on a busy Saturday or a holiday weekend, you may need to reserve a block of hotel rooms for the out-of-towners, so it's a good idea to send out these cards in advance, hoping the feedback will give you an idea of how many rooms to reserve.

Ceremony Program

Although it's technically considered poor taste to provide ceremony programs, I think they add a very special touch to the ceremony. Here are a few reasons why a program is important:

- ∽ It introduces the members of the wedding party and their relationship to the bride or groom.
- ∽ It provides the order of the service.
- ∽ It explains any unusual or creative facets of the ceremony. For example, the fact that the standing wreath of pink roses and baby's

breath is in honor of a recently deceased
family member; or the fact that the bride is
wearing her mother's or grandmother's
wedding gown or veil.

∞ It provides a way to thank those who helped
with the wedding.

∞ It becomes a treasured memento of the
ceremony, not only for the bride, groom,
and their families, but for the guests as well.

A ceremony program can be professionally printed,
along with your invitations, or it may be created on your
home computer, using any cursive or fancy font, then
printed onto parchment or fine linen paper. Once printed,
it can be rolled into a scroll and tied with a ribbon, or folded.
Typically, a program is printed on an 8 1/2 × 11 inch piece
of paper that has been folded in half, resulting in four pages.

You can be as creative as you want with your content,
including photos of you and your maid of honor when you
were kids together; the love poem your fiancé wrote for
you when he proposed; or the story of how your grandma's
wedding veil was lovingly preserved through the years.

Take a look at wedding Websites where you'll find more
details about composing your ceremony program, such as
theknot.com and *dreamweavers.com*. At the dreamWeavers
site, click on The Reading Room where you'll find an ar-
ticle I wrote that contains an example of an actual ceremony program.

Reception Menu

If you're planning a very formal reception, you may want
to have your menu printed on parchment or other fine quality paper, one copy per table, displayed on the table beside

the centerpiece, or one at each place setting, if it's to be a sit-down dinner.

Post-Wedding Announcements

If your wedding will be ultraformal or formal, your wedding announcements should be engraved in the same manner as your invitations. Here is sample wording for a wedding announcement:

Mr. and Mrs. Henry Wellington
proudly announce
the marriage of their daughter
Leanne Marie
and
Mr. Sean Gregory O'Neill
Saturday, the seventeenth of April
two thousand and five
St. John's Episcopal Church
Remmington, Missouri

The person(s) announcing the wedding should be the same names listed on the wedding invitations themselves.

Thank-You Notes

When you place your order with the stationer for your wedding invitations, enclosures, and announcements, order personalized thank-you stationery at the same time. By personalized, I don't mean that your expression of thanks within the thank-you note or letter should be printed, because that is *never* acceptable. Personalizing does mean having your name or monogram engraved on the front or top of the stationery.

Thank-you notes sent by the bride before the wedding should be personalized differently than those sent by the bride and groom together after the wedding. Here are the rules of etiquette, which can be a little confusing, so listen up (there will be a test):

Thank-you notes sent before the wedding should have the bride's monogram (fancy initials) engraved on the front of the notes, in this order:

- ∞ The initial of her surname should be in large font in the center of the monogram.
- ∞ The initial of her first name in smaller font on the left, and the initial of her middle name on the right.

The return address on the back flap of the envelope should be her home address.

Thank-you notes sent by the couple after the wedding should have the couple's monogram engraved on the front of the notes, in this order:

- ∞ The initial of the couple's surname should be in large font in the center of the monogram.
- ∞ The initial of the bride's first name in smaller font on the left, and the initial of the groom's first name on the right.

The return address on the back flap of the envelope should be their new home address.

Note: See Chapter 18 for the rules regarding the writing and sending of thank-you notes.

Wedding Newsletters

Wedding newsletters are becoming quite popular, especially for weddings that involve a large wedding party and out-of-town guests. The idea of the letter, which can be e-mailed, faxed, or snail-mailed to everyone involved during the months preceding the wedding, is to keep them informed of the plans. For example, if the groom is planning a golf day with his attendants, he'll want to let them know when, where, and what to bring for the minitournament. If the bride is planning a spa day for her attendants, she'll want to let her attendants know so they can look forward to the treat.

For out-of-town friends and relatives who may be arriving a week or so before the wedding, or who may be staying in local hotels, it's nice to send them brochures and maps from the local visitors' bureau or chamber of commerce, in case they want to work in a little sightseeing. You'll also want to keep everyone informed of any special family activities you have planned for the out-of-towners, such as an afterglow following the reception (see Chapter 18), or a picnic the day after the wedding.

These newsletters can become quite creative, including such things as a scanned copy of the couple's engagement photo, or a photo of family members at work tying pew bows for the big day. You can also include biographical sketches of each member of the wedding party, which will help them get acquainted when they meet in person at the wedding rehearsal.

> *A popular trend is to establish a personal wedding Website that includes a constantly updated newsletter, gift registry information, hotel reservation forms, an online guest book, a message board for live interactive discussions and planning, plus a wedding photo album page to display your wedding photos after the wedding.*

Out-of-Town Guest Itineraries

It's a nice touch to provide printed itineraries for your out-of-town guests, once they've arrived in town, many of whom may be staying at the same hotel. You can include general information, including interesting places to visit, maps with directions to the ceremony and reception and a timetable of planned events. These itineraries may be computer-generated if you like.

If your out-of-towners will be invited to any special planned events, such as the rehearsal dinner, a round of golf, or a formal tea, you can order printed invitations. Here is an example:

Welcome Brunch
Friday, May 15th at 11 a.m.
at the home of
James and Esther Cunningham
201 West Palmdale Drive
Transportation will be provided from
your hotel by chartered cable car.

If the Wedding Is Canceled

If the wedding is canceled after the invitations have been mailed, the invitations must be recalled by sending professionally printed cards. Sample wording:

Mr. and Mrs. Andrew Morgan
announce that the marriage of their daughter,
Anna Marie
to
Mr. William Farnsworth
will not take place.

Be sure the persons making this announcement are the same people whose names appeared at the top of the original invitations.

Chapter 9

HIRING YOUR PRODUCTION CREW

You can't produce your show without some help, so it's time to hire your production crew. You'll need a producer, a director, set designer, cameramen, stage manager, and costume designers, musicians, and limos for transporting the stars of the show.

This is one of the most important chapters in this book, because your choice of vendors and service providers, and how they perform on your wedding day, will determine the tastefulness of your wedding. For example, if you're looking for a DJ to provide the music for your reception, you want one who will follow the rules of etiquette, not only in the music he chooses to play, but how loud he cranks up the volume, how he's dressed, and how he conducts himself. You don't want one who thinks he's Mr. Showbiz, with his loud, obnoxious manner and crude remarks. You want one who will follow the rules and help establish the tone and character of your reception, providing an elegance and style as he conducts himself in a professional way.

You don't want anything embarrassing or inappropriate to interfere with the elegance and tastefulness of your wedding day, so my goal in this chapter is to help you screen out Mr. Showbiz, Mr. Sloppy Photographer, and Mr. Casual Limo Driver, dressed in wrinkled khakis and a golf shirt. Just because *you* know how to behave on your wedding day, and you know how your *cast members* should behave, doesn't mean *they* know how to behave. So don't assume anything. Just because they're "wedding professionals," it doesn't mean they will act professional. This is why it's so important to interview each vendor and service provider as thoroughly as possible, asking as many questions as you can to ensure that the rules of proper wedding etiquette are followed in every aspect of your wedding.

So, as you audition professionals for your show, you'll need a few guidelines.

The first step, before you meet with any vendors or service providers in person, is to do a little homework. Call the Better Business Bureau (BBB) in your town and your state's Department of Consumer Affairs, to see if they have received any complaints. The next step is to talk to friends and relatives who have either hosted their own weddings, or been guests at weddings, and can pass along their impressions of various dance bands, caterers, and other service providers. If the professionals you have in mind pass these two tests, you're ready to meet with each one in person.

You'll also need to decide on your wedding's formality, because this will help determine who should be considered for each role. For example, if you're planning an ultraformal wedding, you should provide live music, as opposed to a DJ who plays recorded music; a formal sit-down meal should be served, as opposed to a less formal buffet line; and you should reserve an upscale reception venue, as opposed to the social hall located in your church's annex. For less formal weddings, you can bend all these rules considerably, as you'll see throughout this chapter.

The bottom line is this: if you want vendors and service providers to abide by the rules of proper wedding etiquette, you'll need to ask a lot of questions and make your choices very carefully. Then, you must be sure all the answers to your questions, as well as all legal responsibilities, are written clearly into a contract that is signed and countersigned by all parties. This is the only way to ensure that your wedding will be conducted in a tasteful, proper way.

Wedding Coordinator

The first decision you'll need to make, before you hire any vendors or other service providers, is whether you want to hire a professional wedding coordinator, also called a wedding planner, a wedding consultant, or a bridal consultant. If so, look for one who is a member of a professional organization, such as the Association of Bridal Consultants; June Wedding, Inc.; or Weddings Beautiful Worldwide, a division of National Bridal Service.

> *Don't confuse a full-time professional wedding coordinator with an on-site "bridal consultant" or a vendor's employee with the title of "wedding consultant." For example, a church may have a staff member whose mission is to see that you follow the church's guidelines as you plan your wedding. Or, a vendor, such as a florist or a caterer, may have an employee who specializes in weddings.*

If you do hire one of these awesome people to help you plan your wedding, that person will be able to recommend vendors and service providers he or she has worked with in the past. This person will also help you stay within your budget and advise you on wedding etiquette questions. In addition, he or she will help you shop for your bridal gown and attendants' attire, and generally coordinate all your plans. Of course, the most valuable service this person will provide is to keep your wedding day on track.

You'll find that wedding coordinators are paid in a variety of ways:

- ❧ A percentage of the wedding costs.
- ❧ Flat fees based on the services provided.
- ❧ Fees based on the amount of time required.
- ❧ A small fee, plus commissions and/or referral fees from their referred vendors. (The practice of accepting commissions or referral fees is often frowned upon by professional wedding consultant organizations. However, if a professional wedding coordinator does receive compensation from referred vendors, he is obligated to inform his client.)

You may decide to hire a wedding coordinator for the sole task of staying on track during the wedding rehearsal, ceremony, and reception. A person hired for this limited duty is often called a wedding director or a wedding day director.

If you don't hire a professional coordinator, you'll need someone to fill this role. You may have an experienced friend or relative who'll be willing and able to help out. Otherwise, the bride and groom and their parents will need to work together to be sure nothing falls through the cracks, especially during the week before the wedding.

Questions You Should Ask Before Hiring a Wedding Planner

- ❧ Are you a certified member of a professional association?

- How long have you been in business?
- How many weddings have you planned since you became a full-time professional?
- Do you have referrals?
- How do you charge? Are there any extras not included in this fee?
- Do you accept commissions or referral fees from referred vendors?
- When is the deposit due? When are remaining payments due?
- How much time will you spend with us? Before the wedding? During the rehearsal, ceremony, and reception?

It's considered very poor etiquette for a wedding professional to insinuate him- or herself into the wedding festivities, by socializing or flirting with any guests or other wedding professionals present, or by offering a toast to the bride and groom. I know of an actual case where a wedding planner asked someone to be her assistant on the day of the wedding. The planner didn't know this person very well and didn't realize she was a recent divorcee on the make. She arrived in a sexy dress and proceeded to flirt and socialize during the reception. When the reception was over, the wedding planner was appalled to hear her assistant brag how she landed dates with the band director and the divorced father of the groom!

Wedding Officiant

The next member of your production crew is your wedding officiant, who'll serve as your stage manager during the rehearsal, and your script-prompter during the ceremony. Your choice of officiant will depend on whether you're planning a civil or religious ceremony. If you prefer a religious ceremony, you'll not only need to find a church or synagogue that's available on your wedding day, but a clergyman, priest, or rabbi as well.

If you prefer a civil wedding, contact your local city hall or marriage license bureau to locate a county official who is legally qualified to perform the ceremony, such as a justice of the peace, judge, or county clerk. If you're planning a civil or religious ceremony at a secular venue, you'll need to find an officiant who is willing to travel to that venue.

Questions You Should Ask When You Meet With Your Officiant

- Are you available on the dates we have in mind for our wedding, rehearsal, and rehearsal dinner?
- Do you require premarital counseling before you will agree to marry us?
- If we would like a relative or another clergyman to help officiate our wedding, will he be allowed to do so?
- In the case of a previous divorce, are there any restrictions or requirements that must be fulfilled before you will agree to marry us?

- If it is a religious ceremony, will we be required to commit to raising our children in the religious faith involved?

- Will we need to provide our baptism or confirmation certificates?

- Will we be allowed to write our own vows, include a unity candle ceremony, or other variations?

> *If you're planning a civil ceremony at a non-religious venue, your state may issue a special temporary license to a friend or relative to perform the marriage ceremony. To find out if your state issues temporary licenses, contact your local county clerk's office. If so, the temporary license is usually issued by a judge or a county clerk, and will only be valid for a certain number of days.*

Ceremony Site

Your choice of ceremony site will depend on several factors. Do you prefer a civil or religious ceremony? How formal will your wedding be? If you decide on a religious ceremony, will you be required to be married in a house of worship, or will your clergyman, rabbi, or priest conduct the ceremony at a secular site? If the ceremony will be a civil one, will the county officiant agree to marry you at a site of your choosing, or will you be required to be married at the courthouse or other county venue?

Questions You Should Ask
Before You Book Your Ceremony Site

- Can we be married in this place of worship if we are not members of the congregation? If not, can a member sponsor us?

- How many guests will the facility seat? What fees are involved, and do they vary according to the day of the week? (Saturday is the most expensive day of the week to get married.)

- For how many hours will we have access to the site? (Before, during, and after the ceremony.)

- Is any equipment available, and are there fees involved? (Kneeling bench, aisle runner, candelabra, and so on.)

- What services are available, such as church organist, sound system, site wedding coordinator, and so forth? What are their fees?

- Are there restrictions, such as no applause, no contemporary music, no lighted candles, or no flash cameras allowed? Will we be allowed to attach ribbons, floral arrangements, or candelabra to the pews? Note: you may be required to obtain an "open-flame" permit from your city or county in order to have lighted candles.

- Are there restrictions regarding wedding attire, such as yarmulkes must be worn, or bare shoulders are not allowed?

- ∞ Are there any other weddings or events planned the day before, the day of, or the day after our wedding?
- ∞ Are dressing rooms available?
- ∞ Will there be any existing decor available at the time of our wedding? (For example, Easter lilies; Christmas poinsettias; wedding flowers or pew arrangements from another wedding being held the same day?)
- ∞ Are there restrictions regarding photography, videography, and music?
- ∞ Are there restrictions against the throwing of rice, bird seed, or flower petals?

Reception Site

Your reception venue may be near or on the same premises as your ceremony site. If so, this is ideal. Otherwise, the wedding party and the guests will need to be transported to the reception site.

Questions You Should Ask
Before You Book Your Reception Site

- ∞ Is it close to your ceremony site?
- ∞ Does it provide an ambience that's complementary to the style and theme of your wedding?
- ∞ Is it affordable?
- ∞ Is it large enough? The reception site should be large enough to handle:
  - ∞ The wedding party and all your guests.
  - ∞ Tables, chairs, and serving tables required for food and drink service.

- A cake table.
- A guest book table.
- A gift table.
- A receiving line, if applicable.
- A band and dance floor, if appropriate, or space for other musicians or a DJ to setup.
- Separate areas for a wedding arbor or other theme-related decorations.

> *An informal stand-up breakfast or luncheon buffet, or an afternoon tea reception, will obviously require less space than a formal sit-down dinner, followed by dancing and entertainment.*

- May alcohol be served on the premises?
- Does the facility provide liability insurance?
- Is there adequate electrical power?
- How large are the restroom facilities? Are they close to the reception hall?
- Is security staff provided?
- Is a coat check attendant provided?
- If it's an open-air facility, can an alternate facility be provided in case of inclement weather?
- Also, if it is an open-air facility, do they allow the area to be tented or canopied?
- Does the facility have outdoor heaters and lighting?
- Is cleanup included in the fee?

- What is the maximum number of people the room can accommodate?

- Are there musical restrictions? (Size of band, volume?)

- Are any musical instruments available on site? (Piano, organ?)

- How many hours will the facility be available, including time to decorate in advance? Are there overtime fees?

- What equipment is available at the site? (Tables; chairs, linens, and table skirts; utensils; serving dishes; coffee pots; punch bowls; bar supplies; microphone; sound system; and so on.) Are there fees for their use?

- Are there dressing rooms?

- Is there adequate parking and do you provide a parking valet?

- What other events are taking place that day?

- Will there be any existing decor that may be used?

- Will we be allowed to bring in our own caterer, musicians, and so forth? Or, will we be required to order off your menu and hire your servers, bartenders, and musicians?

- If we do provide our own food, drink, and cake, do you charge to cut/serve the cake? Is there a corkage fee per bottle if we provide our own wine or champagne?

- How much deposit is required?

- When is the balance of the money due and payable?

- What is the cancelation/refund policy?

Many reception venues, such as country clubs, hotels, and resorts, require that you order from their menus and hire their food servers, bartenders, setup and cleanup staff, parking valets, and so forth. You may also be required to purchase your wedding cake and champagne from theses facilities, at their prices. Many brides and their families don't mind this idea at all, especially if the bottom line for everything is within their budgets, because they won't need to worry about hiring an outside caterer, chase down discount prices on champagne, or get bids from various bakeries for the wedding cake.

On the other hand, if you want control of your vendors, you'll need to rent a facility that allows you to furnish your own food, drink, and wedding cake, whether you prepare some of the food dishes yourself or bring in an outside caterer.

Popular Reception Venues

- Bed-and-breakfast.
- Botanical garden.
- Community clubhouse.
- Elks hall.
- Farm, ranch, or barn.
- Historical site, such as a library or museum.
- Hotel, resort, or private club.
- Military club facility.
- Museum or art gallery.
- National park facility.
- Novelty site, depending on your theme, such as a zoo, amusement park, ski lodge, apartment-building rooftop, or houseboat.
- Private estate or mansion.
- Private home.

- Private or public garden or park.
- Private patio or poolside.
- Private picnic facility.
- Public beach.
- Restaurant.
- Senior center.
- Social hall provided by your church or synagogue.
- University or college facility.
- Winery.
- Yacht.

> Contact your local Chamber of Commerce and Historical Society for popular sites available in your area. You can also check wedding Websites for links to venue sites in your area.

Stationer

Ask for referrals from friends and recent brides who have been pleased with a stationer's service. Also, look for a stationer who has a large number of catalogs available that include actual samples of the print and paper quality.

Proofread the master copy of your invitation very carefully. In fact, ask a friend to help you—two sets of eyes are better than one. Now is the time to catch any typos or mistakes, *before* the invitations, announcements, and any enclosures are printed.

When your order arrives, proofread *every* word once more, at the stationer's place of business. That way, if you find an error, the stationer can reorder immediately.

> Quality invitations are also available through discount suppliers (look in the advertising sections of current bridal magazines). You can also create the invitations on your home computer, using a wedding invitation kit, for sale at your local arts and crafts or wedding supply store such as Michaels. This kit includes software, a wedding planner, guest list database, and a small supply of invitations, envelopes, and response cards. Additional blank stationery can be purchased at these stores and at office supply stores.

Bridal Salon

You may be one of those lucky brides who walks into a bridal salon, finds the perfect gown with the perfect fit, and walks out of the shop carrying it on her arm. That's not likely, however, which means you'll probably need to place an order for your gown and your bridesmaids' dresses.

To find a reputable salon, ask around for referrals. Disreputable bridal salons don't stay in business for long, so the first thing to look for is one that has been around for a long time.

Once you've decided on the bridal and bridesmaids' gowns, and are ready to place your order, be sure these specifics are included in the contract:

- The gown's manufacturer, style number, size, and color.
- The terms of sale, including the amount of deposit, date of delivery, amount due on delivery, and price quote for alterations, and pressing, if required.

- All extra charges, including storage, delivery, alterations, and taxes.
- Cancelation policy and refund provisions.
- Be sure your contract is signed and countersigned.

> It has become fashionable for the affluent bride to purchase two gowns: one for the ceremony and one for the reception.

Formalwear Rental Store

Personal referrals are the best way to find a reputable formalwear store. Although the groom may decide to purchase his tuxedo, chances are he and the rest of the men in his wedding party will rent them. Once you've decided on the color and style of your formalwear, here are important specifics that must be included in your contract:

- The style, color, and sizes for each ensemble, plus any accessories.
- Specific terms of sale, including the amount of deposit, the date and time the ensembles will be available for pickup, amount due on delivery, and the date and time by which they must be returned.
- Cancelation policy and refund provisions.
- Any extra charges, such as alterations, pressing, storage, and delivery.
- The company's statement of liability, if any of the formalwear is not satisfactory when picked up or delivered, such as a stain, rip, or improper sizing.

∽ Be sure the contract is signed and countersigned.

Caterer and Pastry Chef

The best caterers and pastry chefs have excellent reputations, so, hopefully, you'll receive referrals from a friend or a recent bride who has been pleased with their service.

Questions You Should Ask Your Caterer Before Signing a Contract

∽ How do you charge (per plate or per food item)?

∽ How much food will be provided per guest (get the specifics, such as ounces of chicken per person)?

∽ Will you provide an experienced supervisor to be in charge during the food service?

∽ How will the food be served? Plate service? Sit-down? Buffet style? Food stations?

∽ May we taste the various food items available before we place our order? May we sample the different types of wedding cake you offer?

∽ May we see photos or videos of past weddings that demonstrate your food presentation?

∽ Do you charge a fee for cutting the cake? Per piece? Flat fee?

∽ Do you offer less-expensive menus for the children and the service providers, such as the musicians and the photographer?

- May we see the actual linens, plates, glassware, tableware, and so forth, that you will furnish?

- Will all tables be skirted? (A paper or fabric skirt that wraps the table from tabletop to floor.)

- What type of beverages will you serve? If we provide the wine or champagne, will you charge a corkage fee?

- How many people will you provide to serve the food, tend the bar, clean the premises after the reception, and so forth? How will they be dressed? Are they experienced?

- Is your company bonded and do you carry liability insurance?

- May we see your current health permit?

- Will we be allowed to take all leftover food dishes, plus any opened and unopened bottles of wine or champagne for which we paid?

- When is your deadline for the final guest count?

- What is your total price, including all taxes, gratuities, and any extras?

- When are the payments due? How much deposit is required? What is your refund policy in case of cancelation?

Questions You Should Ask Your Pastry Chef Before Signing a Contract

- What are the total costs for the cake, including delivery and setup at the reception venue?

- Do you require a deposit? When is the balance due?
- What is your policy regarding the return of plastic tier plates, columns, or bridges?
- Will you provide take-home boxes for the top layer and any leftover cake?

Establish a dress code for all vendors and service providers who will be seen by your guests. For example, if you're planning a formal wedding, you don't want your videographer showing up in jeans and tennis shoes.

Florist

An ultraformal or formal wedding requires the highest standards in floral decorations. These standards apply across the board, from the quality of the flowers, to the creative artistry of each bouquet and arrangement. To accomplish this feat, you should hire a professional floral designer.

A less formal wedding requires less expertise, and, if you're lucky, you may have friends or relatives who offer to donate flowers from their gardens. Or, you may be able to purchase flowers from a wholesale discount floral market or through a supermarket floral department. You may also have talented friends who will help turn these flowers into bouquets, boutonnieres, and floral arrangements for your ceremony and reception venues.

If you decide to hire a professional, you'll need to do some research.

Questions to Consider Before Hiring a Professional Florist

- ∞ Have you received referrals from recent brides and grooms?

- ∞ Once you receive several referrals, talk to each florist to get a feel for their professionalism.

- ∞ How does the flower shop feel when you enter it for the first time? Are the displays creative and appealing? Do any of the fresh flowers seem droopy? Does the florist seem harried and rushed? Or, does he take plenty of time to answer your questions in a professional manner?

- ∞ Is the florist experienced? How many weddings has he or she done?

- ∞ Can the florist work within your budget?

- ∞ Can the florist subcontract for extras, such as special lighting, decorative backgrounds and props, or live or silk plants and trees?

Specifics That Must Be Included in the Contract

- ∞ A detailed list of every floral arrangement, corsage, bouquet, boutonniere, and other floral pieces or decorations to be furnished by the florist. (Specify which flowers are not acceptable substitutes, in case your first choices are not available for your wedding.)

- ∞ Itemized costs, total costs, amount of deposits, and the date and amount of the balance due, date, times, and addresses for all deliveries, plus the name of the delivery person who will be responsible for placing the arrangements.

> Instead of working through your local neighborhood flower shop, you may decide to hire a *floral designer*, a person who works exclusively by contract out of his or her private studio. Ask your caterer or wedding coordinator for referrals to one of these specialists.

Musicians

Your choice of musicians will depend on the formality and theme of your ceremony and reception. For example, an informal ceremony may require only a soloist accompanied by guitar, a single pianist, or an organist. Or, a more formal ceremony may lend itself to a trained choir or professional singers and musicians, such as a harpist or violinists.

An informal wedding reception may only require recorded music, a DJ, or a pianist, while a more formal affair will require one or more live bands or orchestral groups. In addition, you may want to hire specialty performers, such as a bagpiper or a string quartet.

Before plunking down the deposit for any musicians' services, ask your friends for referrals, especially recent brides and grooms. Within your circle of friends, or with a little help from your local university's music department, you may be able to locate musicians who will perform for free as recital credit, or for a small gratuity. Otherwise, you'll need to hire professionals.

Questions You Should Ask Before Signing a Contract

- May we audition the group, either during a live performance, or by watching a video? (Are they skilled and professional? Do they dress appropriately? Is their music too loud?)

- Will the musician(s) be willing to play your favorite selections, if they aren't already in their repertoire? (You may need to purchase sheet music for a few selections.)
- Exactly how many hours will they perform at the ceremony and/or the reception? How long will their breaks be, and how many will they take?
- What about their attire, especially if you're hiring a DJ to play recorded music?
- What equipment will the musicians bring with them, such as their own sound system? What equipment will you be required to provide? These requirements are often attached to the contract as a rider.
- How much room do they need?
- What is the total fee? How much deposit is required? When is the balance due?
- What about gratuities? Are they included in the contract price?
- Do they charge for overtime?
- Will the musicians expect to be fed?

Unless you're absolutely, positively, unequivocally sure you can do it without crying or butchering the song, don't plan to sing at your own ceremony. Save it for the reception, when you're not as stressed out.

Photographer

You may have one or more amateur photographers in your family who volunteer to photograph your ceremony or reception. If you decide to go this route, be sure you've seen this person's work. Does it meet your expectations? Is the person experienced and reliable?

If you decide to hire a professional photographer, ask recent brides and grooms for referrals. Once you have a list of possibilities, make appointments with each photographer, preferably at his or her studio.

Questions You Should Ask Before Hiring a Photographer

- May we see examples of recent weddings you've photographed?
- Are you familiar with the latest trends in wedding photography? For example:
  - Lifestyle photography.
  - Black and white photography.
  - Photojournalism.
  - Environmental photography.
  - Progressive photography.
  - Candid photography.
  - Sepia style printing.
  - Airbrushing.
  - Soft focusing.
  - Digital imaging.
- May we see examples of your work using these techniques?
- What type of cameras do you use? What type of equipment will you bring?
- What are the prices of your various wedding packages, and exactly how many photos are included in each? Ask to see the quality of any photo albums included in the packages.

- When will proofs be ready to view, and how long before the final photographs will be delivered? May we purchase the proofs? May we purchase the negatives? Will you also furnish the proofs on a disk so they can be shared over the Internet? Or, do you have a Website where the proofs may be viewed and ordered online?

- When will you arrive at the ceremony site? How many total hours are included in your package prices?

- How many assistants will you provide and what will you wear?

- May we furnish a list of personalized photo requests to be added to your standard list? (You may want a special photograph taken of you and your grandmother, for example.)

- How much deposit is required, and when will the balance be due?

> *Don't hire a photographer unless you feel comfortable with him or her. Some photographers have a drill sergeant personality. It's poor etiquette for your guests to be ordered around by a loud, bossy photographer, so look for one who has a soft-spoken, inoffensive manner.*

Videographer

Most brides and grooms want their ceremony and reception captured on video You may have one or more friends or relatives who offer to videotape your wedding day, and if you're familiar with that person's work, that may be all you need. However, a professional videographer will usually provide a great deal more when it comes to artistry, special effects, and services. For example, a professional usually provides two high-quality video cameras, editing, animated titles, musical enhancements, and, very importantly, fully charged, dependable battery packs!

You may decide to hire one professional, in addition to a few friends who volunteer their services, or you may want a professional as your one and only videographer. If you decide to hire a professional, ask around for referrals. Then, meet with each one individually, to get a feel for the videographer's artistic style, in addition to his or her personality. Again, as with the photographer, it's offensive to your guests and considered poor etiquette for a videographer to be loud and obnoxious. You want one who is subtle and unobtrusive, especially during the ceremony.

Questions You Should Ask Before Hiring a Videographer

- How many video cameras will be in use? What type of equipment will you provide?
- Do you provide wireless microphones for the bride, groom, and officiant during the ceremony?
- Will you be using a digital format?
- Will you have an adequate number of charged battery packs available?
- What are the prices of your various packages, and what do they include?
- What sites will you cover? (Bride's home? Ceremony and reception venues? Other candid photo locations?)

∞ Exactly when will you arrive and when will you leave each venue? (Often the videographer gets tired of hanging around the reception and leaves before the cake cutting, so be sure this person is committed to stay long enough to videotape your cake cutting, plus your getaway at the end of the reception.)

∞ How many hours of (pre-edited) raw footage will you provide?

∞ Will you provide an assistant?

∞ What about attire?

∞ How long will the edited tape(s) be? When will they be ready?

∞ What amount of deposit is required, and when is the final payment due?

Limousine Rental Company

You may decide to hire one or more limousines to provide transportation for:

∞ The bride and her father to the ceremony venue.

∞ The mother of the bride and the bridal attendants to the ceremony venue.

∞ The groom and his attendants to the ceremony venue.

∞ The bride, groom, and their wedding party from the ceremony to the reception. If your ceremony and reception are held at the same site, that simplifies things considerably.

∽ A getaway vehicle for the bride and groom following the reception.

Before Signing on the Dotted Line

Here are a few precautions you should take:

∽ Ask other brides and grooms for referrals.

∽ Visit several rental companies before choosing one. Look for one that has been in business for a long time and is a member of the National Limousine Association.

∽ Look for a company that provides experienced, professionally attired drivers, and whose limos are clean and well maintained. Also, be sure the drivers speak English, if that is your language of choice.

∽ Be sure the contract includes all the details, including the total cost, amounts of deposit and when final payments are due, any added expenses, the make and year of the vehicle being reserved, amenities included, the driver's attire, and refund and cancelation policies.

Final Warnings Before Hiring Any Vendors or Service Providers

∽ Get everything in writing. Even though you may casually discuss and agree on certain incidental items that aren't usually part of a contract, be sure they are written in anyway. It's difficult to come back after the fact and say, "But I remember distinctly that you said your staff would stay to clean up the kitchen!"

If it's not in writing, it's amazing how easily verbal agreements are forgotten.

∞ Be sure all contracts are signed and countersigned. If a vendor or a service provider refuses to sign a contract, don't do business with him or her.

∞ Find out how long a company has been in business. Ask for references.

∞ Ask to see the company's business license.

∞ Don't hire anyone who seems in a rush or talks down to you. If you don't have good feelings about the person or the company, keep looking until you feel comfortable with your choices.

∞ Don't sign anything until you've checked with your local Better Business Bureau and your state's Department of Consumer Affairs. If there's even one complaint filed against a company, take that as a red flag!

Chapter 10

THE WEDDING REHEARSAL

The wedding rehearsal, and the rehearsal dinner that follows, usually take place the evening before the wedding. The time of the rehearsal should be convenient for everyone, especially the officiant. Hopefully, the rehearsal can be held early enough in the evening to allow for a relaxing dinner afterward.

Whether your wedding will be ultraformal or casual, certain rules of traditional etiquette still apply today, especially when it comes to such things as conducting the rehearsal, hosting the dinner, and offering toasts.

A wedding rehearsal is a joyous time, marking the end of many long months of anticipation and tedious planning. Finally, it's time for everyone in the wedding party to meet each other and socialize for the first time.

Purpose

The purpose of a wedding rehearsal is to run through the ceremony, including the processional, recessional, and the order of service. Each member of the wedding party needs to know when to walk, how to walk, and where to stand throughout the ceremony. The bride and groom need to feel comfortable with the officiant and the sequence of events. They also need to know when to speak, when to be silent, and when to move, including such things as lighting the unity candle or circling the altar three times, as required by certain religious faiths.

The musicians, as well as anyone who will recite a poem or read from scripture, also need to rehearse.

The rehearsal is especially important for any children involved in the ceremony, including the candlelighters, junior ushers or bridesmaids, the flower girl, ring bearer, and trainbearers or pages, if the bridal gown's train is long enough to be carried.

If the rehearsal is being held in a house of worship, find out ahead of time if there is a dress code for those in attendance. Some churches don't allow super-casual attire, such as cutoffs, tank tops, or flip-flops, even during a wedding rehearsal.

Who Conducts It?

The officiant usually conducts the rehearsal, along with the wedding coordinator, if you choose to hire one, who will help line everyone up and establish a pace for the processional, and so forth.

Who Should Attend?

Basically, everyone involved in the ceremony should attend, including the officiant, attendants, musicians, bride, groom, their parents, and any other participants.

Etiquette Do's and Don'ts

- ∞ The bride usually carries a pretend bridal bouquet (created from bridal shower ribbons and bows), as she practices walking down the aisle, handing it off to her honor attendant during the ceremony, then retrieving it before the recessional.

- ∞ The bride and groom usually do not recite the actual vows during the rehearsal, but listen to the officiant go over them briefly.

- ∞ The rehearsal should move along quickly, lasting no more than an hour and a half. This should allow plenty of time for the participants to run through the entire service twice.

- ∞ Deliver the marriage license to the officiant for his or her safekeeping. That way it won't be forgotten or misplaced on the wedding day itself.

- ∞ Bring and deliver checks for anyone who is being paid to participate, such as the soloists, organist, or harpist.

- ∞ If trainbearers or pages will be carrying the bridal gown's train, attach or tie a length of fabric to the bride's waist during the rehearsal so the children can get used to carrying it.

- ∞ It's become popular, if you can afford it, to have the photographer and videographer present during the rehearsal and the dinner that follows. Otherwise, ask friends and relatives to bring their cameras and video cameras, plus you can also provide disposable cameras for anyone to use during both events.

Chapter 11

THE REHEARSAL DINNER

The rehearsal dinner traditionally follows immediately after the rehearsal. It can be compared to a cast party after the final dress rehearsal, a time to relax and enjoy each other's company after all the hard work that went into the production.

Who Hosts It?

According to traditional etiquette, the groom's parents should host it. However, in today's spin on wedding etiquette, almost anyone may host it. It may be hosted by the bride's parents, the couple's grandparents or any other relative, or the members of the wedding party. Or, the dinner may be hosted as a joint effort by both sets of parents, the bride and groom, and anyone else who wants to contribute to the cause.

Degree of Formality

A rehearsal dinner for an ultraformal or formal wedding usually follows the same degree of formality as the wedding, often a sit-down, catered dinner. However, with today's lean toward less formal weddings, almost anything goes. It can be a get-together at a pizza place, a picnic in the park, a potluck dinner where several people involved contribute a favorite dish, or it may be an ala carte affair in a private dining room of a nice restaurant.

> The most important thing to remember when planning the rehearsal dinner is for it to have a comfortable setting where everyone can relax, get to know each other, and enjoy each other's company before the big day. If the bride's and groom's relatives haven't met before the rehearsal, it's a nice touch to use place cards so that each relative can be seated next to someone he or she doesn't know.

Who Attends?

The bride and groom attend, of course, plus their parents, grandparents, siblings, and any close out-of-town relatives who have traveled especially to attend the wedding. Also, the attendants and their fiancés, spouses, or live-in companions, along with the parents of any children who are participating in the wedding. The children, if very young, should be left with a babysitter during the dinner, along with something special for them to eat, such as a fast-food kids' meal. The officiant and his or her spouse should also be invited.

It's a good idea for the hosts to mail out invitations to this dinner, so that there will be no misunderstandings or hurt feelings. The invitations don't need to be elegant, especially if the dinner will be pizza or a poolside barbecue. Here's an example:

*You are invited to a buffet supper
at the home of
Mr. and Mrs. Henry Buckingham
1274 North Maple Avenue
Friday, June 17
following the rehearsal
for the marriage of
Sarah Marie Heston
and
Ian Nester Pandet*

Toasts

It's traditional to offer toasts during this dinner. (See Chapter 15 for the suggested order of the toasts.)

Etiquette Tips for the Rehearsal Dinner

- ∞ This is a great time to make introductions all around, affording an opportunity for the extended families of the bride and groom to meet and get to know each other before the wedding.

- ∞ This time together can be a poignant, memorable experience by encouraging family members to relate little stories about the bride and groom when they were young, or possibly presenting a home video or slide presentation, showing the couple as they were growing up.

- If you haven't already presented your attendants with their thank-you gifts during the bachelor party or the bridesmaids' luncheon, this is a good time to do so. It's also a good time for the bride and groom to thank anyone present who helped with the wedding preparations.

- Almost everyone attending this dinner has been under some kind of strain as they prepared for the wedding, so it's a nice touch to follow the dinner with something fun to loosen things up. Depending on the dinner's formality and venue, you might plan a game of volleyball or horseshoes, karaoke, or any other kind of mixer activity.

- It's in poor taste for the groom's parents to host a rehearsal dinner that is far more elegant and formal than the reception meal.

Whoever hosts this dinner should pay for all the food and drink. It's considered poor etiquette to expect the guests to purchase their own drinks at a cash bar.

Chapter 12

THE
CEREMONY

The wedding ceremony is the heart of your wedding day, and you and your fiancé are the stars of the show. As you plan your ceremony, you'll soon discover that it's a major production, with rules of etiquette abound at every turn. If you're not especially fond of rules and restrictions, you might want to avoid a religious or ultraformal wedding, because "religious" and "ultraformal" equate to mandatory rules of strict traditional etiquette that must be followed.

A less formal ceremony, or a civil ceremony that takes place at a secular venue, are much less restrictive. In fact, as the formality of the wedding decreases, the rules slacken to the point of being practically nonexistent for a super-casual wedding, such as a surprise wedding or a novelty wedding on board a hot-air balloon.

In this chapter we'll take a look at all the facets of a ceremony and how etiquette applies, including religious and civil services, ceremony venues, the music, photography, videography, flowers, and decor. We'll also consider poignant special touches you may want to add to your ceremony, plus contemporary alternatives to the traditional wedding.

Religious Ceremony

Most religious groups will furnish you with a list of their wedding policies, plus what is or is not allowed to take place on the premises. So, your first step is to take a look at these requirements before you commit to getting married at a religious venue. Take your time as you consider your options—this is a big decision.

Protestant

A protestant wedding may be more or less restrictive than a Catholic wedding, depending on the denomination. For example, a protestant church wedding is almost never allowed on a Sunday.

If you were married before, this is usually not a problem with most protestant officiants; however, I've heard of several ministers who refuse to marry a couple if one or both have been divorced.

Depending on your clergyman's policy, the wedding may take place in a church or at a secular site.

Seating

The bride's family is usually seated on the left side of the church, and the groom's on the right. The parents are usually seated in the front rows, and brothers, sisters, and their spouses in the second rows on each side. The third rows are reserved for grandparents and other close relatives, followed by additional relatives, and, finally, friends of the bride or groom.

When parents are divorced, the mother is usually seated in the front pew (alone or with her new husband), and the father is seated in the third pew (alone or with his new wife). The rule of thumb is to keep one pew between divorced parents.

In the case of a father of the groom who is married to the mother of the bride, it's best that he not be seated at all, but serve as his son's best man. If his son has already chosen a friend or a brother as his best man, the father may also serve as best man because it's proper etiquette to have two best men.

> *If the bride chooses not to be escorted down the aisle by both her mother and father, the last person seated before the processional will be the groom's mother.*

Processional

The processional takes place in this order:

- ∽ The clergyman (optional).
- ∽ Groomsmen, walking in pairs (optional).
- ∽ Junior ushers.
- ∽ Junior bridesmaids.
- ∽ Bridesmaids, walking in single file or in pairs.
- ∽ Honor attendant (maid or matron of honor).
- ∽ Ring bearer.
- ∽ Flower girl. (The ring bearer and flower girl may walk down the aisle side by side, if you like.)
- ∽ The bride enters on her father's left arm, followed by any pages or trainbearers who carry the bridal gown's train.

If the bride's father is deceased, or if she prefers to have someone else walk her down the aisle, she has several choices: her stepfather, an uncle, a brother, her mother, her groom, or she may walk down the aisle alone. In the case of an encore wedding, the bride may want her children to walk her down the aisle. If the bride is close to her natural father and her stepfather, she may choose one of them to walk her down the aisle, but she should make a point to include her other dad in some way during the ceremony.

Recessional

The recessional follows this order:

- ∞ The bride and groom.
- ∞ The ring bearer and flower girl.
- ∞ The bride's honor attendant.
- ∞ The best man.
- ∞ The bridesmaids and groomsmen, walking in pairs, the bridesmaids on the groomsmen's right arms.

If you provide a guest book for your guests to sign as they arrive for the ceremony, the attendant may stand beside the guest book up until the bride's mother is seated. Then the attendant should be seated, with the hope that any late visitors will see the book and know to sign it before seating themselves in a back row. Also, after the ceremony, transport the guest book(s) to the reception venue so that any guests who didn't sign before the ceremony may do so there. Providing a guest book at the ceremony site is optional, and many couples provide guest books only at their reception sites.

Roman Catholic

If you want to be married in a Roman Catholic church, you'll usually have a preliminary meeting with the priest to find out what is expected. One requirement may be the posting of the banns (a notice of your intention to wed) each Sunday for three weeks before the wedding. Another will probably be premarital counseling, including a discussion of your religious beliefs.

If you were married once before in a Catholic ceremony, you'll be required to receive an annulment from the Church, which may be a complicated, time-consuming procedure, so allow plenty of time to get this taken care of before your wedding date. You may also be required to furnish the priest with a copy of your certificate of baptism or confirmation diploma.

A Roman Catholic ceremony usually takes place in a church or cathedral on a Saturday at noon, and often includes a nuptial mass, or it may take place on a Friday evening or early Sunday morning. However, the Friday and Sunday ceremony may not include a mass.

The processional, recessional, and the seating are similar to those for a Protestant ceremony.

Jewish

The three main branches of Judaism—Orthodox, Conservative and Reform—differ in their requirements. The Orthodox branch follows the laws of the Jewish faith most strictly. The Conservative branch follows the laws less strictly than the Orthodox, and the Reform branch is the most liberal.

Most branches do not allow weddings to take place on the Sabbath or during any holy days, and also require that a Jewish divorce be obtained before a divorced bride or groom may be married. Speak with your rabbi about other stipulations. For example, not all rabbis will perform an interfaith ceremony and usually only the Reform branch will conduct the ceremony in English.

A Jewish wedding may take place in a temple or synagogue, as well as at a secular site, such as a resort or at your reception location, depending on the accepted custom of each particular rabbi.

Seating

If you are being married in a Reform or Conservative Jewish ceremony, the bride's family usually sits on the right side of the temple, the groom's on the left. However, for an Orthodox ceremony, men sit on one side of the temple and women on the other.

Because the bride's mother and father escort her down the aisle, her mother isn't seated prior to the processional, as is common in a Protestant ceremony. The same is true of the groom's mother, if the groom chooses to be escorted down the aisle by both parents.

Processional

A Reform Jewish processional is usually the same as a Protestant processional. However, an Orthodox or Conservative Jewish processional differs slightly by following this order:

- The rabbi.
- The cantor.
- The bride's grandparents, walking side by side with her grandmother on her grandfather's right (optional).
- The groom's grandparents, also walking side by side, his grandmother on his grandfather's right (optional).
- The ushers (groomsmen) walking in pairs.
- The best man, walking alone.

☙ The groom, escorted down the aisle between his parents (father on his left arm, mother on his right).

☙ The bridesmaids, walking in pairs.

☙ The honor attendant, walking alone.

☙ The ring bearer

☙ The flower girl.

☙ The bride is escorted down the aisle between her parents (father on her left arm, and her mother on her right).

Recessional

A Jewish recessional takes place in this order:

☙ The bride and groom.

☙ The bride's parents.

☙ The groom's parents.

☙ The flower girl.

☙ The ring bearer.

☙ The bride's honor attendant.

☙ The best man.

☙ The bridesmaids, each escorted by an usher (groomsman).

☙ The last down the aisle are the cantor and the rabbi.

The Chuppah

Wherever your ceremony takes place, unless you plan to be married by a rabbi of the Reform branch, you'll be required to provide a wedding canopy, also known as a Jewish Chuppah. (A Chuppah is optional for a Reform ceremony.) A Chuppah may be a piece of fabric or a prayer shawl, supported by a pole on each corner. If the rabbi approves, the poles may be decorated with flowers.

The Chuppah is a symbolic tradition representing the new home (or tent) of the bride and groom. Often, the parents stand with the couple under the Chuppah during the ceremony.

While standing under the Chuppah, the Seven Blessings are recited. At the end of the ceremony, the groom crushes a glass under his foot, which is Jewish symbolism for the destruction of the temple in Jerusalem.

> After the recessional, a Jewish couple traditionally disappears into a private room where they eat something before proceeding to the reception. The reason for this custom is that a newly married Jewish couple must take their first meal alone together.

Other Faiths

Every religious faith has certain requirements and traditions for a wedding ceremony. Meet with your clergyman or -woman to find out what your particular church requires. To give you an idea of how varied these services may be, here are a few examples:

Orthodox

Each Orthodox ceremony, whether Eastern, Greek, or Russian, has its own unique traditions concerning the importance of the Holy Trinity, where the couple stands during the ceremony, how the wedding rings are exchanged, the wearing of crowns, and other strict rituals that must be incorporated.

Quaker

The Quaker faith requires that a notice of intent to wed be read at least a month before the wedding, in front of a meeting of the Society of Friends. The ceremony is quite simple and much less ostentatious than other faiths, with the bride and groom seated facing the congregation.

Amish

An Amish ceremony is also quite simple, with no wedding march or musical instruments. One of these ceremonies usually takes place on a Tuesday or a Thursday, following the harvest.

Congregational

A bride and groom are usually expected to be members or regular participants of the congregation where the wedding will take place. This religious denomination places a great emphasis on personalizing the service, with the bride and groom involved in planning the ceremony, including which hymns will be sung and which Scripture will be read.

Muslim

A Muslim ceremony is composed of a contract, a covenant, and mutual affirmation. The historical dowry system is still being used today, with the bride's father presenting the dowry to the groom. The marriage itself becomes public when it is declared during an Islamic service.

Interfaith Ceremony

Interfaith ceremonies are not permitted by all faiths, especially at a place of worship. Many couples opt for a civil ceremony instead, especially in certain cases. For example, it's usually difficult to arrange a wedding in a Jewish synagogue between an interfaith Jewish and Christian couple, although some Jewish Reform rabbis will conduct the ceremony. Also, many priests will agree to co-officiate with a Protestant minister, with a ceremony that includes traditions from both faiths.

If you really want an interfaith ceremony within the walls of a religious venue, you'll need to meet with several officiants until you find one who is liberal enough in his or her thinking to sanction it. In some cases, a religious officiant may agree to preside over an interfaith ceremony if it's held at a secular venue.

Once you've located two religious officiants willing to participate in an interfaith ceremony, protocol requires that the officiant at the ceremony venue is the host and makes the final decisions on what interfaith customs will be allowed. For example, you may want to include customs from each of your faiths, including musical selections, prayers, and scripture readings.

Civil Ceremony

A civil ceremony, also known as a legal ceremony, is usually held at a government office, such as the judge's chambers, or at a secular venue, such as a resort, a private club, a private home, or any other nonreligious site. It's usually officiated by a judge, justice of the peace, or other court official who is allowed to conduct a legally binding wedding in your state.

Although a brief civil ceremony usually follows protocol and phrasing established by the *Book of Common Prayer*, you may be allowed to add to the ceremony with customized vows, prayers, or readings. This will not only lengthen the ceremony, but will personalize it. Most secular officiants prefer to personalize the ceremony for the couple, so ask beforehand.

Military Ceremony

A military wedding usually takes place in a military chapel and is almost always considered a formal affair. The groom wears his dress uniform (white in summer or blue in winter), as do any of his attendants who are also in the military. The most stunning and dramatic part of a military wedding is when the bride and groom walk under arched military swords or rifles as they exit the ceremony venue. Also, the wedding cake is usually cut using the groom's sword.

Here are a few rules that must be followed for a military wedding:

- ☜ The invitations must be worded properly, according to rank (see page 85).

- ☜ The groom, wearing his dress uniform, may wear a sword. If he does so, the bride stands on his right. If not, she stands on his left.

- ☜ If the bride is in the military, she may wear her dress uniform during the ceremony, or she may wear a traditional wedding gown.

- ☜ All guests who wear their military uniforms to the wedding should be seated according to their rank, with the highest rank seated closer to the front, in places of honor.

- ☜ If the groom wears his dress uniform, he may not wear a boutonniere or any other nonmilitary adornment.

Double Ceremony

A double ceremony is one where two couples are married during the same service, usually two sisters or two brothers, or occasionally two cousins or two close friends. This means there may be two groups of attendants and, of course, two brides and two grooms, so you'll need a ceremony venue large enough to hold all these people. In some cases, one group of attendants serves both couples.

In the case of two sisters being married in a double ceremony, the oldest sister is the first to walk down the aisle and the first to be married. The two couples stand at the altar at the same time; however, the oldest bride and her groom recite their wedding and ring vows first, followed by the younger sister and her groom.

Order of Ceremony

The order of your ceremony will depend on whether it's a religious or civil ceremony, and if it is a religious ceremony, you may be expected to follow the dictates of your clergyman, rabbi, or priest. The order of the ceremony differs in each case, but I have included three common orders of ceremony, to give you an idea of what to expect.

Order of Typical Protestant Ceremony

- Prelude.
- Candlelighting.
- Lighting of memorial candle, if applicable.
- Seating of guests.
- Seating of mother of the bride.
- Processional.
- Giving of the bride.
- Prayer.
- Scripture reading.
- Pastoral comments.
- Exchanging of vows and rings.
- Lighting of unity candle.
- Pronouncement of marriage.
- Introduction of the bride and groom.
- Recessional.

Order of Typical Roman Catholic Ceremony

- Prelude.
- Seating of guests.
- Seating of the mother of the bride.
- Processional.
- The priest welcomes the guests.
- Readings and petitions.
- The priest gives a marriage homily.
- The priest asks the couple if they have come freely to marry.
- The bride and groom exchange marriage vows.
- The priest blesses the wedding rings.
- The groom places the bride's ring on her finger.
- The bride places the groom's ring on his finger.
- The priest delivers the nuptial blessing.
- Flowers are given to Mary or to the mothers.
- The nuptial mass begins, if one is included.
- Recessional.

Order of Typical Jewish Ceremony

- Seating of guests.
- Processional.
- The rabbi, the bride, groom, their attendants and parents stand under the Chuppah.
- The bride and groom sip ceremonial wine.
- The bride and groom are blessed by the rabbi.
- The groom gives the bride a gold wedding ring.

- ∽ The marriage contract is read aloud and given to the couple.
- ∽ A family member or guest reads the Seven Blessings.
- ∽ The bride and groom again sip ceremonial wine, which symbolizes their marriage commitment.
- ∽ The groom stomps on a cloth-wrapped glass, as the guests say "Mazel tov."
- ∽ Recessional.

Music

If you'll be married in a religious venue, your musical selections may be restricted, depending on the dictates of that particular religious faith or congregation. If you won't have any restrictions, however, here are popular selections you may consider:

Prelude Music

Adagio from Sonata in E-flat
(Wolfgang Amadeus Mozart)
Air from Water Music (George Frideric Handel)
Arioso (Johann Sebastian Bach)
Canon in D (Johann Pachelbel)
Claire de Lune (Claude Debussy)
Larghetto (George Frideric Handel)
Moonlight Sonata (Ludwig van Beethoven)
Nocture in E-flat, Op. 9, No. 2 (Frederic Chopin)
"O Perfect Love," (Cole Burleigh)

Prelude to the Afternoon of a Faun (Claude Debussy)
"The Wedding Song" (Paul Stuckey)
"Three Times a Lady" (Lionel Ritchie)
Trumpet Tune (Henry Purcell)

Processional / Recessional Music

Aria in F Major (George Frideric Handel)
Bridal Chorus from Lohengrin (Richard Wagner)
Fanfare, Te Deum (Gustave Charpentier)
Jesu, Joy of Man's Desiring (Johann Sebastian Bach)
March in C (Henry Purcell)
Ode to Joy (Ludwig van Beethoven)
Royal Fireworks Music (George Frideric Handel)
Sheep May Safely Graze (Johann Sebastian Bach)
Spring, The Four Seasons (Antonio Vivaldi)
Trumpet Voluntary (Jeremiah Clarke)
Wedding March from *A Midsummer Night's Dream* (Felix Mendelssohn)
"Wedding Processional" from *The Sound of Music* (Richard Rodgers)

Ceremony Music

"All I Ask of You" from *The Phantom of the Opera* (Andrew Lloyd Webber, Charles Hart, and Richard Stilgoe)
"Flesh of My Flesh" (Leon Patillo)
"God Gave Me You" (Ralph Kaiser)
"Grow Old With Me" (Mary Chapin Carpenter)

"Hawaiian Wedding Song" (Al Hoffman and Dick Manning)
"O Perfect Lov"e (Joseph Barnby)
"The Bridal Prayer" (Roger Copeland)
"The Greatest of These Is Love" (Roberta Bitgood)
"The Wedding Song" (Paul Stuckey)
"Two Candles" (Sonny Salsbury)
"What I Did for Love" (Marvin Hamlisch)
"Wither Thou Goest, I Will Go" (Mabel Martin)

> If you have a very special musical selection you want included, but the musicians aren't familiar with it, purchase the sheet music and provide it to your musicians or soloist. Of course, you'll need to clear it through your clergyman first, but chances are there should be no problem.

Photography / Videography

Most photographers restrict using a flash on their cameras during the ceremony itself, except when taking a photo of the bride as she enters the venue on her father's arm, and of the bride and groom as they exit the venue after the ceremony. During the remainder of the ceremony, a photographer usually takes timed photos from the balcony, or some other inconspicuous spot.

The videographer may tape the entire ceremony, also from inconspicuous spots within the venue. If there are two people videotaping the ceremony, one camera will usually be mounted on a tripod in the back or on the balcony. The other camera may tape from the front of the venue.

It's considered poor etiquette to keep your guests waiting at the reception site while you're having photos taken at the ceremony site. One popular solution is to plan as many pre-ceremony photos as possible. To pull this off, you'll need to arrive at the ceremony venue in plenty of time for these important pre-ceremony photos:

- The bride with her attendants.
- The bride with her parents and siblings.
- The groom with his groomsmen and ushers.
- The groom with his parents and siblings.
- If the bride and groom don't mind seeing each other before the ceremony, *all* the formal photographs can be taken beforehand.
- If the bride's or groom's parents are divorced and don't want to be photographed together, simply have them each photographed separately with the bride, groom, or wedding party. This will require more poses, more expense, and more time to assemble the various poses, but it may be necessary in the case of hostile parents.

Until you do arrive at the reception venue, keep your guests happy with a cocktail hour or hors d'oeuvre and beverage service.

Flowers

Flowers, along with your other site decorations, will create a certain ambience for your grand production, much like a movie set or stage scenery. A good rule of thumb when it comes to wedding etiquette is that the more formal the wedding, the more profuse and elaborate the flowers should be. For example, for an ultraformal wedding, the bride usually carries a large, elaborate, cascading bouquet and the floral displays are elegant and oversized. Or, an informal wedding may only require a bridal corsage and one flower arrangement.

Your wedding coordinator and/or your floral designer will offer suggestions. A simple venue may need more floral arrangements and decorations than an exquisite cathedral, whose stained glass windows and existing ornamentation may require less elaborate arrangements.

A poignant touch is for the bridal bouquet to contain her groom's boutonniere, which she pulls out and pins on him after she reaches the altar.

Bridal Bouquet Styles

Today's brides have a great deal of leeway when deciding on the style of their bridal bouquets. The most popular bouquet styles are described below. If you're planning an ultraformal or formal wedding, a cascading bouquet, arm bouquet, or clutch bouquet will be the most appropriate. Otherwise, any style is suitable, whether the bouquet is assembled professionally, or you make your own bouquet with fresh or silk flowers.

Cascading Bouquet

This bouquet is assembled in a vertical shape that falls below the bride's waist, usually with long knotted ribbons that trail down.

Arm Bouquet

This bouquet consists of six or eight long-stemmed flowers, tied with ribbons and carried in the crook of the arm.

Clutch Bouquet

This term is applied to any small rounded bouquet "clutched" tightly to the waist, such as a nosegay.

Wrist Bouquet

This is a small round pomander-shaped bouquet, suspended from the bride's wrist by a ribbon or decorative cord.

Additional Bouquet Possibilities:

A White Bible or a Prayer Book

Top the Bible or prayer book with a single white orchid and streaming ribbons.

Round- or Heart-Shaped Wreath

Cover the wreath with wide white satin ribbons. Add narrow trailing ribbons and one or two silk or fresh flowers.

Tussie-Mussie Bouquet

If you're planning a Victorian wedding, fashion a simple tussie-mussie bouquet by hand-tying the stems of several dainty fresh or dried flowers with ribbons. Insert the stems into a silver or white tussie-mussie cone, which can be purchased at your local floral or wedding supply store.

Sheaves of Wheat

If you're planning a Greco-Roman or medieval wedding, the bride may carry sheaves of wheat tied with a white ribbon. This simple idea also works well for any informal wedding that takes place in an outdoor setting.

Candy Cane

For a holiday wedding, the bride may carry a large decorated candy cane. Use typical greenery to embellish the candy cane, such as holly, mistletoe, or sprigs of evergreens.

Tie the candy cane with a large red bow sprinkled with gold or white sparkles.

Note: Any of these ideas may be adapted for bridesmaids' bouquets, boutonnieres, and mothers' corsages. Floral wreaths or individual flowers are also appropriate for the bride's, attendants,' or flower girl's hair.

> It's perfectly acceptable to transport your ceremony flowers to your reception site, unless your wedding is on a Saturday and your religious venue requires that all wedding flowers remain for the Sunday service. Also, if there are two weddings planned on the same day at the same site, it's fine for the two families to split the costs of the floral decorations, if suitable, for both weddings.

Decorations

The decor should be compatible with the formality of the wedding and the size and number of the floral arrangements. The more formal the wedding, the more elaborate and upscale the decorations should be.

For example, an ultraformal wedding is usually decorated with genuine satin ribbons, as opposed to acetate ribbon which may be used for a less formal wedding. Also, a formal wedding may embellish the aisle ends of each pew with tall silver candle stands, decorated with large satin bows and real flowers. However, a less formal wedding may only require a small acetate bow attached to the pew itself. Also, silk flowers may be used in the arrangements and other floral decorations, in place of real flowers.

If you're planning an ultraformal wedding, you should employ a floral designer, a professional who works out of a studio, instead of using a standard retail florist. Consider this person to be your *set designer*, an artistic specialist who'll coordinate all your site decorations, including the flowers. A less formal wedding, however, may be decorated beautifully with less expensive flowers, ribbon, and other decorations.

Special Touches

Depending on your ethnic or cultural backgrounds, you may want to incorporate a few traditions into your ceremony or reception. The trend these days is to deviate as far as possible from the boring "cookie cutter weddings" of the past and plan around a theme, ethnic customs, or personalized special touches.

> Take a look at my books, *How to Have a Big Wedding on a Small Budget*, 4th Edition and *Diane Warner's Wedding Question and Answer Book*, for detailed information on dozens of wedding themes.

Bride and Groom Face the Guests

The bride and groom switch places with the officiant, which means they're facing the guests. This helps the guests feel more closely involved in the ceremony.

Bride's Tributes to the Mothers

The bride carries two long-stemmed roses with her bouquet as she walks down the aisle. Before reaching the altar, she kisses her mother on her cheek as she presents her with one of the roses. Then, following the ceremony, the bride presents the second rose to her new mother-in-law, also with a kiss on the cheek. Another variation to this tribute is for the bride to present the mothers with individual flowers pulled out of her bouquet.

Jumping the Broom

This is a lovely African-American tradition dating back to the 17th century. By jumping over the broom at the end of the ceremony, the bride and groom are symbolizing their love and commitment to each other as they establish a new beginning and a home of their own. It's common to decorate the broom with flowers and ribbons.

Something Old, Something New

The bride wears something old, something new, something borrowed, something blue, and a sixpence (or a penny) in her shoe. This ancient tradition is still honored today, although most brides haven't a clue where this came from or what it means. *Something old* symbolizes continuity from generation to generation, such as Grandma's lace handkerchief, a piece of lace or ribbon from your mother's or grandmother's wedding gown or veil, or a piece of jewelry that has been handed down in the family. *Something new* symbolizes a glorious, happy future for the bride, such as her wedding gown, veil, gloves, or any piece of jewelry. *Something borrowed* symbolizes joy and happiness, such as your sister's pearl necklace or earrings, your mother's gloves, or a friend's lace handkerchief. *Something blue* symbolizes fidelity and love, such as a blue lace garter, a blue ribbon sewn into the bride's petticoat or woven into the bridal bouquet, blue lingerie, or a blue sapphire ring. *Sixpence in her shoe* assures the bride that she'll be happy and lucky throughout her marriage.

Handfasting

This is an ancient Celtic marriage ceremony that has become especially popular since it was included in the movie *Braveheart*. The bride's right wrist is tied to the groom's left wrist during the ceremony. This is symbolic of the couple's commitment and devotion to each other. This is where the popular phrase originated: "Tying the Knot."

Orange Blossoms

The bride wears orange blossoms in her hair. Orange blossoms have been symbolic of fertility and a happy marriage for centuries, going back to Greek and Spanish tradition. She may wear a cluster of orange blossoms, attached to the top of her veil or behind an ear, or she may wear a wreath of orange blossoms.

Salted Bread and Grain

The bride sews salted bread into her petticoat and the groom carries grain in his pocket. This is an old German custom that assures future wealth and good luck.

Silk Cord

The bride and groom are wrapped with a silk cord during the ceremony. This touching Mexican custom is symbolic of the joining of the bride and groom, to become one. The cord is wrapped over the couple's shoulders in a figure eight.

Lighting of the Unity Candle

This tradition has become quite popular in the last 10 years or so because of its deep meaning. After the bride and groom have recited their vows, they walk together to the unity candle, which is a large candle that sits unlighted between two smaller lighted candles that represent the two families. The bride and groom each lift a smaller candle and, together, light the larger unity candle, symbolizing their marriage to each other and that two families have become one.

A variation of this ceremony is for the parents of the bride and groom, or any children of the couple, to participate. The bride's parents and/or children help hold the bride's candle as the flame is used to light the unity candle. The groom's parents and children do the same.

Covenant of Salt

A salt ceremony, as it's sometimes called, is a meaningful addition to a wedding service. The bride and groom each hold a bag or glass container of salt. These containers of salt represent their individual lives, with all they were, all they are, and all they will ever be. The bride and groom willingly empty their containers of salt into a larger container, symbolizing the joining of their lives for eternity. Just as the grains of salt can never be separated and returned to their individual containers, so the couple is now no longer two, but one, never to be separated one from the other.

Memorial Tribute

Memorial tributes have become extremely popular. For example, a bride may display a small floral wreath on a stand beside the altar as a tribute to her father who recently passed away. Or, the groom may include a written tribute to his grandfather in the ceremony program. The couple may light a special candle in memory of a loved one, or the bride or groom may carry or wear a memento that belonged to the loved one. This memento may be mentioned in the ceremony program.

Personalized Wedding Vows

Most brides and grooms prefer to recite personalized vows, instead of traditional vow phrasing, such as these traditional words sometimes recited during a Roman Catholic wedding mass:

"I, _____, take you, _____, for my lawful wife/ husband, to have and to hold, from this day forward, for better, for worse, for richer, for poorer, in sickness and health, until death do us part."

Here's a sample vow of creative, personalized vows, taken from my book, *Diane Warner's Complete Book of Wedding Vows*:

"I bring myself to you this day to share my life with you. You can trust my love, for it's real. I promise to be a faithful mate and to unfailingly share and support your hopes, dreams, and goals. I vow to be there for you always. When you fall, I will catch you; when you cry, I will comfort you; when you laugh, I will share your joy. Everything I am and everything I have is yours, from this moment forth and for eternity."

Isn't this touching? I love personalized vows!

Here's another example, taken from the chapter called "Vows With Religious Variations":

"Before God brought you into my life, I walked alone; now I have you at my side and we walk together. You are my strength and my priceless treasure. I cherish you, adore you, and thank God for you. Just as the Bible says that God dwells in us and his love is perfected in us, so God knew us both and chose us from the beginning of time, to share as one and to be one...one life, one love, one heart. I welcome you, _____, as my husband/wife, and I promise with God's help to be your faithful husband/wife, to love and serve you as Christ commands as long as we both shall live."

Here's a religious example, taken from the chapter called "Vows Inspired by the Classics":

"Sensual pleasure passes and vanishes in the twinkling of an eye, but the friendship between us, the mutual confidence, the delights of the heart, the enchantment of the soul, these things do not perish and can never be destroyed. I shall love you until I die." (Voltaire)

In my book, *Diane Warner's Complete Book of Wedding Vows*, you'll find hundreds of personalized vows and vow phrasings, included in chapters such as "Vows With Religious Variations," "Ring Vows," "Vows Inspired by the Classics," "Vows for Older Couples," "Vows for Second Marriages," and "Vows That Include Children." Also included in the book are two more popular special touches: the Rose Ceremony and the Wine Ceremony. (See Chapter 17 for examples of vows for second marriages and vows that include children.)

Ring the Bells

The bride and groom ring the church's bell together after the ceremony. This is a lovely tradition, letting everyone in the community know that the ceremony is over and that the couple is overjoyed to become one.

Tip for the bride: Discourage having visitors in your dressing room before the ceremony. According to traditional etiquette, only your attendants and the two mothers should be with you before you walk down the aisle. However, in today's everything-goes world, guests who perceive themselves to be special feel they have the right to stop by and wish you well before the ceremony. Bad idea! This is not the time for the bride to be receiving guests. Being swamped with well-wishers is also dishonoring to the mothers who should be given the special privilege of being with the bride during this time. So, here is a case where I cling to tradition! Lock the dressing-room door!

Dove Release

If you're planning a daytime wedding, you may want to consider a dove display and release. White love doves have always been symbols of holiness, love, and fidelity. They may be displayed in a cage during your wedding reception. Then, as you make your get-away, the doves are released into the sky.

Contemporary Alternatives to the Traditional Wedding

The traditional wedding ceremony and reception are often replaced by contemporary alternatives, such as the destination wedding, progressive wedding, surprise wedding, all-night, weekend, or totally casual wedding. The reasons couples opt for one of these alternatives is because they are less expensive, more convenient, less stressful, or because they're more practical for their family.

Destination Wedding

A destination wedding, also called a honeymoon wedding or a travel wedding, is a wedding that takes place at the honeymoon site. Various resorts specialize in all-inclusive wedding/honeymoon packages, including many in the Pocono Mountains of Pennsylvania, in Hawaii, the Caribbean, Mexico, and, of course, Las Vegas, Nevada.

The key is to find a hotel or resort that provides an experienced, on-premise, full-time wedding coordinator who arranges everything for you, all for one set price. Many of today's couples opt for this type of wedding because it's usually much less expensive than it is to pay for a separate wedding, reception, and honeymoon. Also, the couple will know in advance exactly how much everything will cost, so there aren't any unexpected financial surprises as the wedding day draws near.

The bride and groom may be accompanied to their honeymoon site by their best man and maid/matron of honor, plus their parents. Or, if the honeymoon site is fairly easy and affordable to reach, close friends and family members may be invited. If travel is out of the question for friends and family members, most resorts and hotels that specialize in destination weddings furnish witnesses for the wedding, which is a great solution.

By the way, many destination wedding venues, especially Las Vegas resorts, have adopted the latest electronic technology, which allows them to show a wedding live over their Website. This is an ingenious way for your friends and family to watch your wedding on their computer screens back home. Many couples even send wedding invitations, inviting their guests to "come to our wedding on the Internet."

> If your honeymoon venue doesn't provide a wedding coordinator, it's imperative that you hire an independent professional in the city where your resort is located. Ask the resort's concierge for referrals to experienced professionals in the area.

Weekend Wedding

The trendy weekend wedding is one part family reunion, one part vacation for the guests, and one part wedding. Usually, the weekend begins with a Friday evening get-together hosted by a family member, which includes a cocktail welcome party, the wedding rehearsal, and the rehearsal dinner. The guests are entertained during the day on Saturday with a barbecue picnic, a poolside party, or sports activities, such as golf tournaments and tennis matches. The wedding and reception are held on Saturday evening, followed by a full day of activities on Sunday, including such things as a brunch or a sightseeing tour around the city.

Progressive Wedding

A progressive wedding takes place over several days. It's the most complicated and expensive type of wedding to plan. There may be two ceremonies, one in the bride's hometown, one in the groom's, plus a series of receptions that may take place in several cities. A progressive wedding is a wonderful idea for a couple who has close friends and family members living all over the state, many of whom want to host their own reception for the couple.

Surprise Wedding

Surprise weddings are also becoming popular options to the full-blown ceremony and reception. By "surprise wedding," I don't mean that it's a surprise to the bride and groom—only to most of those in attendance. The wedding may take place during a family reunion, a holiday get-to-gether, a New Year's Eve party, or any other get-together where friends and family already plan to attend.

All-Night Wedding

An all-night wedding is exactly what it says: a wedding that's celebrated all night long, finally ending with a sit-down breakfast or breakfast buffet. The ceremony may take place at the reception venue, such as a resort or hotel, or it may take place at a separate venue. In either case, the guests party all through the night with eating, drinking, dancing, and in some cases, they may crash for a while in a suite of rooms that have been reserved for the guests.

When refreshed, they wake up, drink a little coffee, and keep going. This type of wedding celebration is perfect for a New Year's Eve wedding, with the ceremony taking place around 11 p.m., followed by cocktails and hors d'oeuvres until midnight when the real party begins.

Novelty Wedding

A novelty wedding is one that's extremely casual, affordable, and uncomplicated—just the opposite of a progressive wedding. One of these weddings may take place at the top of a ski slope, in a hot air balloon, or at any other unique venue. Many of today's couples opt for this kind of simple wedding, surrounded only by their closest friends and family members. A novelty wedding is obviously less expensive than a large, traditional wedding, but that isn't the only reason why they've become popular. Often the bride and groom just want to *get married* and they don't have the time, money, or energy to plan a huge affair.

Chapter 13

THE RECEPTION

Your wedding reception will be a joyous affair that celebrates the success of the grand production at your ceremony site. However, it will be more expensive and complicated to plan than your ceremony. In fact, a wedding reception usually accounts for 50 percent of a wedding's total budget. This means that if you plan to spend $20,000 for everything, your reception will probably cost around $10,000.

Proper wedding etiquette should be followed as you plan your reception, depending on its formality. An ultraformal affair must follow the strict rules of traditional etiquette; however, less formal receptions may incorporate many of the contemporary twists. For example, traditional etiquette dictates the precise structure of a receiving line, but contemporary etiquette allows great liberties, including such things as a novelty groom's cake and unusual specialty entertainment.

> It's fashionable to have two receptions. First, a simple cake and punch reception for all your guests, served immediately after the ceremony. Then, later in the day, a smaller, but more elaborate, reception for close friends and family members.

Reception Venue

Your first step is to find a venue that's not only afford-able and suitable for your reception's theme and formality, but also available on the date you have in mind for your wedding. As you begin your search, you may find that your favorite venues are already booked, so you may need to set your wedding date according to when your favorite venue is available.

Another important consideration is whether a recep-tion venue requires that you order your food, drink, and wedding cake from them. For example, most restaurants, hotels and resorts will not let you bring in your own caterer, or provide your own wedding cake or champagne. How-ever, other venues will allow you to have total control, such as historical sites, museums, and other city and state facilities. This means you can save money by shopping around for an affordable caterer, providing some of the food dishes yourself, purchasing your champagne by the case from Costco or any wholesale warehouse, or accepting your aunt's generous offer to make your wedding cake.

Take a look in Chapter 9 for important questions you should ask before booking any of your wedding vendors or service providers.

Degree of Formality

According to traditional etiquette, a formal wedding ceremony should be followed by a formal reception. How-ever, according to contemporary rules of etiquette, it's quite acceptable for a formal ceremony to be followed by an in-formal reception.

Your reception's formality will also depend on the re-ception venue. For example, an upscale resort, country club, or hotel ballroom are formal settings, whereas a public park, high-rise rooftop, or a ferryboat are less formal venues.

If your reception is ultraformal or formal, you'll be expected to have a receiving line. You'll also be expected to serve your guests a sit-down (plated) luncheon or dinner, as opposed to a buffet-style meal or a simple cake and champagne reception, which are perfectly acceptable for a less formal affair. An ultraformal reception also requires live music, as opposed to a DJ or other recorded music.

Style or Theme

The style or theme of your reception may follow that of your ceremony, or it may have its own personality altogether. For example, you may have an elegant, formal traditional wedding ceremony, followed by a rowdy Mardi Gras reception. Or, you may have a casual wedding and reception that take place at the same venue, such as a park, a beach, or Grandma's backyard.

Flowers

The more formal the reception, the larger and more elaborate the floral decorations will need to be. For example, an ultraformal or formal wedding reception will probably include some of these options:

- A large, exquisite floral centerpiece for the bride's table.
- Smaller, yet elegant, arrangements for each guest table.
- Arbors and arches decorated with greenery and fresh flowers.
- Decorated topiary trees.
- Fresh flowers on the cake and/or the cake table.
- Small flowers attached to the place cards.
- Tall, free-standing floral arrangements framing doorways and the cake table.

ℂ Garlands of greenery, ribbons, and fresh flowers intertwined in and around food displays on the buffet table or the food stations, and draped over doorways and windows.

As the formality of the reception decreases, so do these expectations. For example, a semiformal wedding reception may only need a nice centerpiece for the bride's table, plus the bridesmaids' bouquets displayed on the bride's table or around the base of the wedding cake. The flowers for an informal reception may be as simple as large clusters of lilacs from Grandma's garden, or rented baskets filled with silk mums and gladioli.

> It's perfectly acceptable to transport ceremony arrangements to the reception site—that way they serve double duty, and your guests will think you splurged on both sites.

Decorations

In addition to the floral arrangements, the rest of the decorations should be comparable in their formality.

Here are some popular options:

ℂ Tall, tapered candles or floating votive candles.

ℂ Gold (brass) or silver candelabra.

ℂ Lots of tulle, lace, and ribbon, tied into bows, trailed along the tables, or clustered around candles or centerpieces.

ℂ Strings of tiny white lights, draped around indoor plants and outdoor trees or bushes.

- ∞ Paper lanterns.
- ∞ Decorative screens.
- ∞ Rented statuary.
- ∞ White or wrought iron benches.
- ∞ Carousel horses.

Table Settings

An ultraformal or formal wedding reception usually requires a sit-down meal. Therefore, the guests are seated around tables. A semiformal or informal wedding reception only needs clusters of chairs placed around the venue, assuming the guests will be served finger foods, appetizers or hors d'oeuvres.

Assigned Seating With Place Cards

When guests are seated around tables, it's considered proper etiquette to provide place cards, so the guests will know where to sit. In addition to the guests' tables, there should be a head table, sometimes called the bride's table, where the bride and groom are seated, along with the members of their wedding party. The bride and groom sit at the center of the table, the best man beside the bride, and the bride's honor attendant beside the groom. The groomsmen and the bridesmaids sit alternately, boy-girl-boy-girl, on each side of the best man and bride's honor attendant.

The bride's table is usually one long rectangular table with everyone seated on one side facing the guests. In the case of an exceptionally large wedding party, the bride's table may be arranged in a U-shape, with the opening of the U facing the guests. A round bride's table is also popular, because the wedding party can see each other and easily carry on a conversation.

> *If your wedding party is small, you may want to include each attendant's spouse or date at the head table. Otherwise, the spouses and dates may be seated together at a table as close to the head table as possible.*

Other tables should be designated for the couple's parents, grandparents, and other relatives, especially those who have traveled from out of town. The parents' table should include both sets of parents, plus the officiant and his or her spouse. If your parents are divorced, or divorced and remarried, seat them at separate tables with relatives from their sides of the family. Also, take care to separate feuding friends, divorced parents, or other relatives, assigning them to tables as far apart as possible.

Give careful thought to the seating of the rest of your guests as well, clustering them in groups according to their ages and interests. It's a good idea to involve both mothers in this planning. Here are a few helpful suggestions:

- ❧ Designate a table for out-of-town relatives who haven't seen each other in a long time and want to visit.

- ❧ Designate one or more tables for single adults.

- ❧ When seating couples, always alternate the men and women around the tables, keeping the couples separate.

- ❧ Seat older guests as far from the music as possible.

- ❧ Even though you're planning a short stand-up reception, *always* provide seating for elderly, disabled, or pregnant guests.

If you don't provide a place card for each guest, you can assign someone the task of informing your guests where they are to be seated as they arrive at the reception venue. This can be done easily by making up an alphabetical guest list ahead of time with a table number beside each name. If you choose this option, be sure the table numbers are tall enough to be seen by the guests as they scan the room.

Table Decor

The tables should be decorated according to your theme, your wedding colors, and the formality of your reception. For example, if your reception theme is Mardi Gras, the table may be decorated with bright colors, including confetti, helium balloons, and masks. Or, if it's an elegant, formal affair, your tables may be decorated with exquisite orchids and long tapered candles in silver candlestick holders. If your wedding colors happen to be raspberry and pale pink, cover the tables with matching linen cloths and napkins and place complementary floral arrangements on each table.

According to traditional etiquette, an ultraformal or formal wedding reception requires that the tablecloth and napkins be linen, and the tablecloth to drop to the floor. The plates should be fine China, and the glassware, crystal. The tableware will usually be sterling silver, although silver-plated is fine.

A less formal reception allows for relaxed rules and more creativity when it comes to table decor. You may use paper or plastic tablecloths, standard plates and glasses, and stainless steel tableware. If it's a very casual reception, such as a backyard barbecue/pool party, use disposable tableware.

> *Floral centerpieces should be higher or lower than the eye-level of the guests. Otherwise, they'll interfere with guests' conversations.*

Place Settings

An ultraformal setting includes:

- A server plate, aka *charger plate*, must be set at each place. The first course is set on top of this plate.
- Silverware should be placed as follows: To the left of the plate, working out, are the salad fork, meat fork, and fish fork. To the right of the plate, working out, are the salad knife, meat knife, fish knife, and soupspoon. Above the plate, working up, are the dessert fork and dessert spoon, placed horizontally.
- The crystal glasses should be placed as follows: A small sherry glass above the soupspoon. Above the forks, working up, are two pairs of glasses. First, the water glass on the left and a red wineglass on the right. Then, a white wineglass on the left and a champagne glass on the right.
- The dinner napkin is placed on top of the charger plate.

A formal or semiformal setting includes:

- One dinner plate in the center of the setting and one bread plate above the dinner fork.
- Silverware should be placed as follows: To the left of the plate, place one dinner fork. To the right of the plate, working out, are a dinner knife and a soupspoon. Above the plate, working up, are the dessert fork and

dessert spoon, placed horizontally. A bread knife should be rested horizontally across the bread plate.

∽ A trio of crystal glasses should be placed above the soupspoon: a water goblet, which is placed closest to the spoon, plus red and white wineglasses, which stand side by side above the water goblet.

∽ The dinner napkin is folded and placed in the center of the dinner plate.

A setting for a less formal meal, or for a buffet-served meal includes:

∽ One bread plate to the upper left of the setting.

∽ No center plate.

∽ Silverware should be placed as follows: To the left of the plate, one dinner fork. To the right of the plate, a dinner knife. Above the plate, working up, are the dessert fork and dessert spoon, placed horizontally. A bread knife should be rested horizontally across the bread plate.

∽ One water goblet is placed to the upper right above the place setting.

∽ The napkin may be folded and placed in the center of the setting, although there is no center dinner plate.

Order of the Reception

A typical wedding reception lasts about three hours. If your reception is scheduled to begin at 2 p.m., this is a workable timetable:

2 p.m. The master of ceremonies announces the members of the bridal party as they walk through the entrance of the reception venue, with the bride and groom the last to enter. If you plan on having a receiving line, it's usually formed immediately. It's nice to have beverages and hors d'oeuvres served to your guests as they wait to join the line.

> Try to keep your post-ceremony photography as short as possible so you don't keep your guests waiting for more than 30 to 40 minutes before you arrive. One way to pull this off is to take as many pre-ceremony photographs as possible. Another idea is to take all photos that include the bride's parents first. That way they can arrive at the reception in time to greet the guests and assure them that the rest of the wedding party is on its way.

2:40 p.m. The clergyman or reception host asks a blessing on the meal.

2:45 p.m. The bridal party is seated at the bride's table, where they are served by waitstaff as the guests line up for the buffet or are served a sit-down meal.

3:30 p.m. After everyone has eaten, the musicians play for the couple's first dance, followed by other traditional pairings, and finally by the rest of the guests (see the dance order on pg 190).

4 p.m.   The musicians stop playing as the best man offers the first toast, followed by other toasts (see Chapter 15 for the toasting order).

> The best man has the option of offering his toast before the meal is eaten, but if he does so, he must be sure everyone has been served a toasting beverage.

4:15 p.m.   After the toasts, the best man or the host invites the guests to gather around the cake table for the cake-cutting ceremony. The cake is then served to the guests.

> It's always best to cut the cake earlier rather than later, because some of the guests may leave after two hours or so. If you're planning a reception that will last longer than three hours, schedule the cake-cutting for two hours, or less, after the reception has begun.

4:30 p.m.   Time for the bride's bouquet throw and the groom's garter toss.

4:45 p.m.   The bride and groom slip away to change into their traveling outfits and say private good-byes to their parents, while the musicians continue to play and, hopefully, the guests continue to dance, visit, and enjoy themselves.

5 p.m.   The bride and groom dash through a shower of birdseed, rose petals, or bubbles, tossed or blown over them by the

wedding guests, as the couple jumps into their getaway car and zooms off to their honeymoon. The guests may return to the reception venue, if they like, for a little more dancing and socializing.

> *Although it's traditionally considered poor etiquette for the bride and groom to stay until the end of the reception, contemporary etiquette allows them to stay as long as they want. When you do leave, be sure all the guests know, so they can give you a proper send-off.*

Master of Ceremonies

The bride's father or the groom's best man usually serves as the master of ceremonies. Or, you may have a couple who agrees to serve as host and hostess of the reception, in which case the host will serve as master of ceremonies. In some cases, the DJ or the bandleader may assume this responsibility.

If the bride's father is the official host of the reception, it's common for him to welcome the guests as soon as everyone has arrived from the ceremony site and gone through the receiving line, if you have one. By "official host," I mean the person whose name appears at the top of the wedding invitation, which, according to traditional etiquette, is the person hosting the reception. In addition to welcoming the guests, the reception host, whoever he is, also announces the best man's toast, the beginning of the cake-cutting ceremony, the bouquet toss, and the couple's departure.

In general, the host should see that everything flows along according to schedule, so that the reception ends at a designated time. As you can see by the suggested timetable given above, it's important for everything to click right along, or the reception will drag.

It'll be easier for the host to keep things flowing if he furnishes copies of the timetable ahead of time to the best man, musicians, caterers, entertainers, photographer, and videographer.

Preferably, the reception host or master of ceremonies, should not be a loud, obnoxious comedian who dominates the affair. I'm sure you've seen this type of character—one of those people who loves to hog the microphone and constantly ham it up. The MC's job description is to make announcements and keep things moving along on schedule, using a moderated voice, sans the stand-up comedy routine.

Guest Books

You can provide one or two traditional guest books, usually placed on a table near the entrance to the reception venue. These books are attended by friends who are dressed in attire that's complementary to the wedding colors, and wear a corsage or boutonniere.

Popular alternatives to traditional guest books are wedding day diaries. These are bound books with blank pages, or single sheets of paper that are placed at each reception table for the guests to write on. The guests may wish the couple well, recall happy childhood memories, or say something clever or humorous. Be sure the parents and members of the wedding party sign the guest books as well.

It's also fashionable to display the engagement photograph with an extra-wide matte for the guests to sign.

Receiving Line and Other Options

A receiving line is required for an ultraformal or formal wedding; otherwise, it's optional. If you do decide to have a receiving line, allow 30 or 40 minutes for every 200 guests. If you have more than 200 guests, you can speed things up by limiting the receiving line to only the bride, groom, and both mothers.

You may form the receiving line immediately following the ceremony at the ceremony site, or you may form it as soon as the bridal party arrives at the reception venue.

Another alternative to the traditional receiving line is for the guests to remain seated at the ceremony site until they are personally greeted and dismissed by the bride and groom. The guests remain seated after the ceremony until it's time for their row to stand and file past the bride and groom, hugging, kissing, and wishing them well as they exit their pews.

A fourth option is for the bride and groom and the rest of the bridal party to float around the reception venue, visiting briefly with each cluster or table full of guests. This can take place before the first dance, but after the bridal party has eaten. Most guests prefer this option, because they don't have to stand in a long line. If you choose this option, be sure all the guests are seated at their tables so that no one feels left out.

Whether you greet your guests during the receiving line or as you visit clusters of guests during the reception, proper etiquette says they may *congratulate* the groom, but never the bride. The bride should receive *best wishes*, or the guests may tell her how lovely she looks and how they enjoyed the ceremony. In response, the bride and groom only need reply with, "Thank you. I'm so glad you came."

Traditional Order

If you do have a receiving line, this is the traditional order, starting with the first person in the line:

- Mother of the bride.
- Father of the groom.
- Mother of the groom.
- Father of the bride.
- Bride.
- Groom.
- Maid or matron of honor.
- Bridesmaids.

Fathers May Sit Out

It's perfectly acceptable for the fathers to sit out. This is a wonderful way to speed up the receiving line, especially if there are more than 200 guests. If the fathers do opt out, they should spend the time socializing with the guests who are not queued up to go through the receiving line.

If Parents are Divorced

If the bride's or groom's parents are divorced and have not remarried, the fathers should sit out altogether. This eliminates the awkward situation where a divorced couple must stand together in the line.

If Divorced Parents Have Remarried

If divorced parents have remarried and you would like to incorporate stepparents into the receiving line, this is the order, if the bride's father has divorced and remarried:

- Bride's mother.
- Groom's father.
- Groom's mother.
- Bride.
- Groom.

- ෨ Bride's stepmother.
- ෨ Bride's father.

(and so on)

If this is an awkward situation, don't include either father or the stepmother in the receiving line.

Wedding Gifts

Traditional wedding etiquette requires that all wedding gifts be delivered to the bride's home before the wedding day. However, in this day of contemporary wedding etiquette, this rule is rarely followed, and it's common for guests to show up at the reception carrying a wrapped gift. Also, certain cultures and ethnic groups expect that all the guests will bring their gifts to the reception. In any case, you'll need to provide an attractive gift table where the gifts may be placed.

It's never proper to open the gifts during the reception. It's also in poor taste to display previously opened gifts. Provide a decorated box with a slit in the top for wedding cards, especially those that may contain cash or a check. It's also a good idea to provide paid security or have a trusted friend keep an eye on the gifts and the card box. Unfortunately, well-dressed thieves know how to crash a wedding reception unnoticed and walk away with gifts or the card box.

Be especially careful not to display any checks on the gift table—not only is this considered very poor etiquette, but they're awfully tempting.

> Have someone assigned to attend the gift table. That way, as each gift is placed on the table, the gift attendant can tape the card securely to the gift. It's a sinking feeling to return from your honeymoon, all primed to open your wedding gifts, only to find a pile of gifts with no cards attached.

Food and Drink

An ultraformal wedding reception requires a formal, elaborate sit-down (plated) dinner at an upscale venue, preceded by a cocktail hour, although non-alcoholic beverages may be served in lieu of traditional cocktails. It's especially important to plan a cocktail hour if you know the post-ceremony photos are going to take an hour or more.

> If possible, plan to have the cocktail hour at an attractive venue adjacent to the reception site, such as a rose garden or a veranda.

Guests should be given a choice of entrée. For example, if you plan to serve chicken, beef, and fish, ask for your guests' preferences on the response cards enclosed with the wedding invitations. That way you'll have an idea how many guests prefer each of your entrées.

If you don't ask for guests' preferences beforehand, you can have your caterer prepare several different meat selections, plus a vegetarian alternative. That way, your guests make their choices at the time of service. If you decide to take this route, the most important factor is to be *sure* you plan on more guests choosing the vegetarian dish than you might expect. It's also a good idea to provide alternative choices for any guests who are allergic to shellfish, nuts, lactose, or other foods and additives. Ask your caterer for his advice.

A formal reception allows for either a sit-down or buffet meal, also at a similar venue. If you serve a buffet meal, however, it's a nice touch to place individual salads at each place setting before the buffet service begins. This is a nice balance between a fully plated meal and buffet-served food.

A semiformal reception calls for much lighter fare, such as a light luncheon or a finger-food buffet, served at a nice, but less formal venue. An informal reception allows for more homespun hospitality, including dishes prepared by friends and family members, a barbecue, or a light finger-food or dessert-only buffet table.

The amount and type of food served will depend on what time your reception will take place. It costs less to feed guests certain times of day. As a rule of thumb, you're required to serve a full meal only if your reception takes place during a regular mealtime. Otherwise, you can get by with much lighter fare. Here are guidelines:

9 a.m. to 11 a.m.	*A full breakfast or continental breakfast buffet.*
11 a.m. to 1 p.m.	*A brunch buffet.*
Noon to 2 p.m.	*Sit-down or buffet-style luncheon.*
2 p.m. to 5 p.m.	*Tea reception with light hors d'oeuvres or tea sandwiches.*
4 p.m. to 7 p.m.	*Cocktail reception with finger foods and appetizers.*
7 p.m. to 9 p.m.	*Sit-down or buffet-style dinner reception.*

If you decide to have a cocktail reception with finger foods and appetizers, it's a nice touch to have your hot or cold hors d'oeuvres butlered, aka tray-served, where servers roam around the venue *butlering* food to each group of guests.

Beverage Options

You have several beverage options, depending on your budget and the formality of your reception. Here they are, starting with the most expensive:

Open Bar

An open bar means that your guests may order drinks of their choice at your expense throughout the affair, from the time they arrive until the bar is closed an hour or so before the end of the reception.

Tray Service

Tray service is when waiters or waitresses walk around the venue offering guests pre-poured drinks carried on trays. This is less expensive than providing an open bar because you have control of the type and amount of beverage being served, the times when these drink trays will be passed, and when this service will stop. Normally, drink trays are passed when the guests arrive, before the meal is served, and, finally, right before the toasts are scheduled to begin.

Bottles of Wine on Each Table

You may supply every table of eight guests with two bottles of wine: one red wine and one white. This should provide one glass of wine for each guest with the meal, and a refill as the toasts begin.

Beer and Wine Only

If you're planning an informal or a casual reception, provide kegs of beer and cases of a good quality wine. This will keep costs down and make your guests happy at the same time.

Serve Champagne Only to the Wedding Party

This is a popular option where the wedding party is served champagne and the rest of the guests are served a less expensive beverage. Although this idea is popular, it's actually in poor taste. If you can't afford champagne for the wedding party *and* all the guests, serve a less expensive beverage to everyone.

Self-Service Punch Bowls

Unless your wedding is ultraformal, punch bowls are quite proper. Most receptions offer two kinds of punch, one that contains alcohol and one that does not. Obviously, fruit punch is much less expensive than an open bar or tray service, plus the amount of alcohol consumption can be controlled according to the ratio of champagne to fruit drink. It's also easy to cut off the supply of alcohol an hour or so before the end of the reception by refilling the punch bowls with non-alcoholic beverages.

It's also acceptable to have a *dry reception*. That is, no alcohol served at all, in which case a non-alcoholic beverage is used for the toasting. By the way, if the word gets out that you're planning a dry reception, don't be surprised if Uncle Charlie, or some other guest, shows up with a flask. If this happens, alert the reception host so he can keep an eye on the obnoxious fellow.

> It's *never* acceptable to have a cash bar (a bar where the guests are expected to order and pay for their drinks). A cash bar is in very poor taste, because wedding guests shouldn't be expected to pay for any part of attending a wedding and reception.

How to Display the Food

Unless the meal is served as plate service at a sit-down meal, the food is usually displayed on a buffet table or at food stations. Food stations are separate tables, each serving a different type of food. For example, you may have a cheese and fruit table, a hot hors d'oeurve table, a prime rib table (where a chef stands carving), beverage table, and so forth. Each table is decorated with a tablecloth, centerpiece, candles, or other theme-related decorations, depending on your reception's formality.

According to traditional rules of etiquette, only two things are required at a wedding reception: a wedding cake and a toast to the bride and groom by the best man. Everything else is actually optional.

Serving of the Guests

If the food is served from buffet tables or food stations, it's proper for the waitstaff to prepare plates ahead of time for everyone at the bride's table. Once the bride's table has been served, the rest of the guests may serve themselves.

If the food will be served at the guests' tables, plates are prepared for the guests in the kitchen, then served by waitstaff, beginning with the parents' and grandparents' tables. Then, relatives sitting together should be served, followed, finally, by the rest of the guests.

In lieu of plate service (where the plates of food are prepared in the kitchen and placed in front of each guest), you may opt for:

Service a la russe, where the waiters present serving platters of food to each guest, who serves himself.

Family-style service, where large platters or dishes are placed on each table, which allows each guest to serve himself.

French service, where the food selections are placed on linen-covered carts which are rolled to each table. The waiter then serves each guest individually from the serving platters or dishes.

Wedding Cakes

Your wedding reception should have one or more wedding cakes. The bride's cake is the only required cake, and it should be the showpiece of your reception venue. You may also have a groom's cake.

Bride's Cake

What we usually think of as the *wedding cake* is actually called the *bride's cake*. It should be large enough to serve every guest who would like a piece. It should be noted, however, that not all guests will eat cake at all, for any number of reasons—they're diabetic, on a diet, too full from eating the meal, or, believe it or not, some people don't *like* cake.

The cake is usually displayed on a separate table designated as the *cake table*. This table may be decorated with flowers, and it may also provide mints, along with small plates upon which the cake will be served. The bridesmaids' bouquets may be placed on the cake table as decorations, arranged around the front of the table, facing toward the guests.

The cutting of the cake should be an important element of the reception. Many formal wedding receptions, especially evening affairs, provide a dramatic Fairmont Cake Presentation. This is a presentation where the venue is darkened and the cake, which has been kept hidden, is dramatically spotlighted as it's rolled out from the kitchen. There's usually a drumroll, or the band may play a loud fanfare, such as "Here Comes the Bride." Sparklers are often inserted into the top of the cake and lighted just before the cake is rolled out, creating a spectacular presentation.

The bride's cake may be cut immediately after a sit-down meal has been served and eaten. Or, if lighter fare is served on a buffet table or at food stations, the cake is usually cut near the end of the reception, right before the bouquet throw and garter toss.

This is the traditional cake-cutting sequence:

- ☜ Your groom should place his right hand over your right hand as you cut into the bottom layer. You then feed bites of cake to each other.

- ☜ After you have fed each other, you should each cut and serve individual slices of cake to your respective in-laws, the bride serving the groom's parents, and vice versa.

> *The cake smash is one of my least favorite things. Not only is it terrible etiquette, but it just seems silly to smash cake into each other's faces after spending so much time and money on the elegant affair. You can take this with a grain of salt, but if I had my way there would never be another cake smash.*

- ☜ When the bottom layer has been served, cut the next layer up in the same way, from the outside in to where the next layer begins.

- ☜ Continue cutting in this same sequence until you reach the top layer. Then, return to the bottom layer.

- ☜ The top layer is often saved, frozen, and brought out to celebrate the couple's first wedding anniversary. If you choose this option, the cake will need to be triple-wrapped and placed in freezer bags, or it won't last a year.

> A breakfast reception requires a wedding cake, but it can be a light one filled and topped with fruits, such as berries, and served with sherbet or whipped-cream topping.

Groom's Cake

You don't see a groom's cake at many receptions these days, unless you're in the South where they're still popular. A groom's cake is usually a dark cake, such as chocolate or fruitcake.

Traditionally, the cake is cut, boxed up, and presented to each single woman present, which she places under her pillow that night, hoping to dream of the man she's to marry.

According to contemporary etiquette, however, the cake may be cut and eaten during the reception, along with the bride's cake. Or, the cake may be cut and boxed ahead of time to be presented as wedding favors to the guests as they leave the reception. If you decide to cut the groom's cake and serve it to the guests during the reception, it should be cut *after* the bride's cake.

A popular twist is for the groom's cake to symbolize his hobby. For example, if he's a football fan, the cake may be in the shape of a football, with icing "laces." Or, if he's into soccer, it may be in the shape of a soccer ball.

> Save several slices or the top layer of the groom's cake, so that it can be frozen and brought out on your first wedding anniversary, along with the top layer of the bride's cake.

Additional Desserts

In addition to the cakes previously mentioned, cookies and candy are often served. In some cases, the reception is a *dessert-only reception*, at which the desserts, plus tea, coffee, and champagne are the only items served. This type of reception is sometimes called a *tea reception*, which takes place mid-afternoon when a full meal is not expected. A dessert reception usually provides a smaller wedding cake, along with an array of specialty desserts, such as chocolate eclairs, cream puffs, or fruit-filled cookies.

> Be prepared to feed the service providers, including the musicians, photographer, and videographer. You aren't required to feed them the same meal as the guests, but you do need to provide filling, though less expensive, fare. For example, you may serve sandwiches, chips, fresh fruit compotes and cookies. Be aware that some of the service providers may have a clause in their contract that requires they be provided with a full meal.

Music

When planning an ultraformal or formal wedding reception, you should provide live music, such as one or two dance bands or an orchestra to play in a formal ballroom. A semiformal wedding allows a choice between live music and a disc jockey, and an informal wedding may use recorded music or no music at all.

A daytime reception that doesn't require dancing, such as a brunch or tea reception, may require only one or two musicians to play background music. For example, you may hire a harpist or a pianist to play classical selections.

You may also provide additional forms of musical entertainment during the reception. For example, as guests arrive and are waiting to go through the receiving line, you may provide music by a string quartet, harpist, or a pianist playing classical or semi-classical selections.

> *Your wedding reception is not a concert, so, except for rowdy ethnic or novelty selections, keep the volume down on the music so guests can socialize with each other.*

Dance Order

Dancing isn't a required activity during a wedding reception. It's fine to have a dance band play only as entertainment. However, if you do decide to include dancing, this is the traditional dance order for a wedding reception:

- ∞ The bride and groom dance the first dance, usually to their favorite song.
- ∞ The bride dances with her father.
- ∞ The groom dances with his mother.
- ∞ The bride dances with her new father-in-law and the groom dances with his new mother-in-law.
- ∞ The bride dances with the best man, and the groom dances with the bride's honor attendant.
- ∞ The bridesmaids and groomsmen join in, dancing with each other.
- ∞ All the guests join those already dancing.

> *If there are more bridesmaids than groomsmen, or vice versa, the odd man or woman out can dance with his or her spouse or date.*

Here are favorite musical selections for these dances:

Bride and Groom's First Dance

- "All I Ask of You" from "The Phantom of the Opera" (Andrew Lloyd Webber, Charles Hart and Richard Stilgoe)
- "Annie's Song" (John Denver)
- "Beautiful in My Eyes" (Joshua Kadison)
- "Because You Love Me" (Celine Dion)
- "Can You Feel the Love Tonight" (Theme from *The Lion King* by Elton John and Tim Rice)
- "Could I Have This Dance?" (Wayland Holyfield and Bob House)
- "Endless Love" (Diana Ross and Lionel Ritchie)
- "Everything I Do, I Do for You" (Bryan Adams)
- "Grow Old With Me" (Mary Chapin Carpenter)
- "I'll Always Love You" (Taylor Dane)
- "It Had to Be You" (Isham Jones and Gus Kahn)
- "Just the Way You Are" (Billy Joel)
- "Living Inside My Heart" (Bob Seger)
- "Looking Through the Eyes of Love" (Marvin Hamlisch and Carole Bayer Sager)
- "My Heart Will Go On" (Theme from *Titanic* by James Horner and Will Jennings)
- "Our Love is Here to Stay" (George Gershwin)
- "So Glad You're Mine" (Al Green)

- "Stand by Me" (Ben E. King)
- "The First Time Ever I Saw Your Face" (Ewan MacColl)
- "Tonight I Celebrate My Love for You" (Michael Masser and Gerry Goffin)
- "Unforgettable" (Irving Gordon)
- "We've Only Just Begun" (Richard Carpenter)
- "Wonderful Tonight" (Eric Clapton)
- "You Are So Beautiful" (Bruce Fisher and Billy Preston)
- "You Are the Sunshine of My Life" (Stevie Wonder)

Father/Daughter Dance

- "Butterfly Kisses" (Bob Carlisle)
- "Daddy's Little Girl" (Al Martino)
- "My Girl" (William Smokey Robinson and Ronald White)
- "My Heart Belongs to Daddy" (Cole Porter)
- "Sunrise, Sunset" from *Fiddler on the Roof* (Sheldon Harnick and Jerry Bock)
- "Thank Heaven for Little Girls" from *Gigi* (Jay Lerner and Frederick Loewe)
- "Thanks for the Memory" (Leo Rubin and Ralph Rainger)
- "The Times of Your Life" (Paul Anka)
- "You Are So Beautiful" (Bruce Fisher and Billy Preston)

> If the bride is close to both her father and her stepfather, one of the fathers may begin the father/daughter dance, then the other cut in before it's over.

Mother / Son Dance

- "I Wish You Love"
  (Lee Wilson and Charles Tenet)
- "My Mother's Eyes"
  (Wolfe Gilbert and Abel Baer)
- "Summer Wind"
  (Henry Mayer and Johnny Mercer)
- "Wind Beneath My Wings"
  (Jeff Silbar and Larry Henley)
- "You Are the Sunshine of My Life"
  (Stevie Wonder)

Ethnic Dances

- The Horah (Israeli folk dance)
- Celito Lindo (Spanish-Mexican dance)
- The Highland Fling (Scottish folk dance)
- The Irish Jig (Irish folk dance)
- The Tarantella (Italian folk dance)
- The Handkerchief Dance
  (Greek folk dance)
- The Dollar Dance
  (European tradition where money is pinned on the bride's gown or the groom's jacket, in payment for the privilege of dancing with him or her.)

> *Ask your reception host, bandleader, or DJ to make a special announcement introducing the music your parents chose for their first dances at their wedding receptions.*

Photographer and Videographer

Your photographer and videographer should be as unobtrusive as possible, capturing poignant candid moments with as many close-ups of the bride and groom as they can get. For example, the couple's faces during their first dance, the bride as she bends to hug her grandmother, or the groom as he embraces his brother after he's delivered the best man's toast.

The videographer may also include interviews with several members of the wedding party, plus family members and guests, asking open-ended questions, such as, "When did you first meet the groom?" or, "How does it feel to be losing your little girl today?"

Traditional posed shots will be on the menu for the photographer as well, including the cake-cutting ceremony and the tossing of the bouquet and garter, but the most poignant memories in years to come will be the spontaneous, candid moments captured on film, DVD, and VHS.

> *Place one disposable camera on each table for the guests to use, taking candid shots spontaneously throughout the reception. (The guests should drop these cameras in designated baskets as they exit the venue.) After you return from your honeymoon and you're reliving your wedding day, these candid photos may provide some of your favorite memories.*

Toasts

The best man's toast is the only one that's required at a wedding reception, although toasts may also be offered by the fathers, the bride and groom, the bride's honor attendant, and other friends and relatives.

Take a look in Chapter 15 for more about these toasts, including an example of a well-constructed toast by a best man. You'll also find important rules of toasting etiquette.

Throwing of the Bridal Bouquet

Traditionally, the bride tosses her bridal bouquet backwards over her head to a group of single women. The woman who catches the bouquet is thought to be the next to marry. Many brides today prefer to keep and preserve their bridal bouquets, so they toss a smaller, less expensive silk bouquet instead, or they have the florist design a bridal bouquet that contains a small throwaway bouquet that can be removed for the bouquet toss.

Some brides dispense with this tradition entirely. Others present the bouquet to their mother, grandmother, or to the woman present who has been married the longest.

Tossing of the Garter

The bride or her groom removes a garter from her thigh, which the groom tosses backwards over his head to a group of single guys. The one who catches it is said to be the next to marry. Many couples are dispensing with this tradition as well.

Special Touches

Personalize your wedding reception by including unique theme-oriented favors, creative entertainment, and a festive send-off as you make your getaway.

Wedding Favors

Traditional wedding favors are small gifts given to the women and girls present, although many favors today are given to all the guests. Although they aren't a requirement, they add a nice touch to the reception. If you can't afford boxes of Godiva chocolates or silver framed photos of the bride and groom, you may be able to afford personalized seed packets, net-wrapped coated almonds, tiny tree saplings, bottles of bubble blowing liquid, silk flower leis, or personalized Christmas ornaments, depending on your theme.

If your reception has an ethnic theme, provide complementary favors, such as Chinese fortune cookies, Irish shamrock cookies, or decorated German chocolate cupcakes.

If you decide to forego favors altogether, you can simply provide candies at each table instead. For example, sprinkle chocolate kisses around the centerpieces.

The Bride and Groom's Getaway

Traditionally, guests have showered the bride and groom with rice as they make their getaway from the reception site. However, because many venues don't allow guests to throw rice, many lovely new customs have emerged, such as blowing bubbles toward the couple; ringing bells; waving lighted sparklers; tossing rose petals; or releasing helium balloons or love doves.

Answers to Sticky Etiquette Problems That May Arise

Here are a few ugly problems that occasionally rear their heads during a wedding reception. You, as the bride and groom, won't need to deal with these problems if they occur, but someone will.

Guests Who Drink Too Much

If you control the amount of alcohol being consumed during the reception, this shouldn't become a problem. As I mentioned earlier in this chapter, there are several ways to do this. Providing two bottles of wine or champagne per table of eight guests is one way to accomplish this feat. Another way is to have all alcoholic beverages served by the waitstaff with tray service, which can be limited to three total servings during the reception. And, of course, the spiked punch bowl can be tamed down with non-alcoholic refills during the last hour of the reception.

In spite of all your precautions, if guests become intoxicated by the end of the day, it's the responsibility of the host to see that they don't drive themselves home. The host, or a family member, may be able to arrange a ride for them, or you may need to call a taxi. But, whatever you do, don't let your intoxicated guests get behind the wheel. If they cause an accident after leaving your reception, you can be legally responsible.

Guests Who May Use Drugs

If you know that certain guests have used illegal drugs in the past, especially when partying, pass the word that this behavior is not welcome during your wedding reception. Then, have a few reliable relatives or friends keep their eyes open during the reception, checking out the restrooms and any guests who seem to be disappearing from time to time. It's sad that you need to police your own party, but, again, just as with an intoxicated guest, you are responsible to be sure he or she doesn't drive.

Enforcing a No-Smoking Requirement

If your reception is being held at a venue that doesn't allow smoking, or if you just prefer a non-smoking reception, there are two things you can do. The first is to provide signs directing guests to a designated outdoor smoking area. Another is to remove all ashtrays from the venue, which will give your guests a clue.

Tasteless Toasts

Once a tacky toast has already been made, there's not much you can do. However, if it's possible, try to anticipate this disaster and head it off before it happens. For example, if you sense that a guest has had a little too much champagne and suddenly thinks he's a *really* funny guy, don't let him get hold of the microphone. Or, if you sense a toast is on its way to becoming pretty raunchy, relieve the guest of the mike before the punch line!

Children Causing Havoc

Even though children may not be invited to your wedding, you can be sure several children will be on hand anyway. This can become a huge problem if small children are running around the reception venue, snatching olives off the buffet table and generally acting out. The solution to this problem is to anticipate it by setting aside a separate room or corner in which the children can play, color, and eat kiddie food that has been prepared especially for them. Of course, you'll also need to provide a couple of babysitters to ride herd on this potentially rowdy little group.

If you're able to reserve a separate room just for them, your sitters can show them kids' videos, play games, and oversee their own little party. Don't assume that all parents will jump at the chance to have their children whisked off to a separate room. If parents prefer to keep their children close, that's fine; at least you've given the parents the option.

> If a parent, sibling, or other close relative dies close to the wedding date, you may decide to go ahead with the ceremony and cancel the reception altogether, or if you decide to have the reception, it should be a more subdued celebration. For example, you may decide to cancel the dance band, eliminate the dancing and any specialty entertainment you had planned.

Chapter 14

Wedding Legalities

Movie stars deal with legal issues all the time, and, as stars of your own show, you'll need to do the same.

The first legal issue you'll need to face is the question of a prenuptial agreement. I know it's not a very romantic concept, but have you and your fiancé given any thought to this idea? And what do you want to call yourself after you're married? Do you want to take your husband's name or keep your maiden name? And, how about wedding insurance? What is it and why do you need it?

Prenuptial Agreements

A prenuptial agreement is a marriage contract between you and your fiancé that you both sign before you get married. It explains the rights and benefits that will exist during the marriage and—heaven forbid!—after the marriage in the case of a divorce. Many couples think that a pre-nup is only for the rich and famous, or for couples who were married before and have complicated financial issues. Actually, every couple can benefit from a pre-nup contract, whether you've been married before or not, and it's proper etiquette for either of you to broach the subject first.

Here are a few of the most important factors addressed in one of these agreements:

- After you're married, how will you take legal ownership of property owned by each of you beforehand, including real estate, stock portfolios, summer homes, and other investments?

- What about business interests?

- How do you handle inheritance payments, alimony, or child support payments?

- How will assets be accumulated during your marriage—jointly or individually?

- Which one of you is responsible to pay any debts accumulated before the wedding?

- How about debts accumulated after the marriage?

- What about life insurance provisions, pensions, IRAs, and 401k accounts?

- In case of divorce, how will your joint assets be divided?

> *Be forewarned that prenuptial agreements do not always hold up in court.*

Marriage License

A marriage license isn't necessarily a simple little document you can walk in and pick up on your way to work. Depending on your state or county, you'll need to fulfill certain requirements, such as:

- Apply together in person.

- Be accompanied by a witness who is at least 18 years of age, and who knows both of you.

- Proof of satisfactory blood tests.

- Birth certificate and/or proof of citizenship.

- Proof of residence.

- May need to provide the date of the wedding and the name and address of the locations and of the officiant

- If underage, your parent(s) may need to give their consent to the marriage.

- If widowed, you may need to produce a death certificate.

- If divorced, you may need to provide a divorce decree.

- Once you've obtained your license, there will usually be a required waiting period before you can marry. The license may only be valid for a certain length of time, so don't apply too far ahead of your wedding date.

Your wedding license must be signed by two people who witness your marriage ceremony who may or may not be your best man and honor attendant. Once you and your witnesses have signed the wedding license following the ceremony, it's the responsibility of your officiant to mail it for recording. Once the wedding license has been recorded, an official copy won't necessarily be mailed to you automatically. You may need to request an official copy in order to legally change your name on your driver's license, social security card, bank accounts, and on other documents.

If you plan to be married outside the United States, it can become even more complicated, so you'll need to find out exactly what will be required. For example:

- Is an original birth certificate required or is a copy acceptable?
- Will you be required to provide them with your driver's licenses and passports?
- How much processing time is required before you can be issued a marriage license?
- Is there a waiting period after the license has been issued?
- Are there religious rules or restrictions, especially in regard to a previous divorce or annulment?
- What fees are involved?

Religious Marriage Certificate

In addition to the marriage license, you may also be required to sign a marriage certificate or contract, depending on the requirements of your religious faith. For example, an Orthodox or Conservative Jewish wedding is not valid until the couple signs the Jewish marriage contract. Other religious faiths have similar contracts, including the Quakers, Amish, and Mennonite denominations, some of which are signed by all the guests present.

Name Changes

You have a decision to make—what will your legal married name be? Traditional etiquette has been tossed out the window, resulting in many contemporary options:

- Add your husband's last name to your last name. For example, if you are Cynthia Marie Roberts and you're marrying Elton Eugene

Wellington, you will become Cynthia Roberts Wellington. By the way, 90 percent of today's brides take their husbands' surnames.

∽ Hyphenate your two last names, becoming Cynthia Marie Roberts-Wellington.

∽ Keep your maiden name as your professional name, but take your husband's last name as your legal name. For example, your business cards may say: Cynthia Marie Roberts, but your bank account may say Cynthia Roberts Wellington.

You, as the groom, have two choices:

∽ Keep your legal name as is.

∽ Change your name by hyphenating your wife's and your last names. For example, if your name is currently Elton Wellington and your fiancée's is Cynthia Marie Roberts, your new name may become Elton Roberts-Wellington.

Once you've decided on your names, you'll need to make changes to the following:

∽ Driver's licenses.

∽ Bank accounts.

∽ Credit cards.

∽ Pension and Social Security records.

∽ Insurance policies.

∽ Car registrations.

∽ Tax records.

∽ Passports.

∽ Property and investment ownership.

∽ Voter registrations.

∽ Wills, living trusts, and powers of attorney.

> Take a look in Chapter 17 for name change options for the bride who has been widowed or divorced.

Wills and Other Financial Issues

When you marry, you'll probably want to change the provisions in your will, especially if you have children from a previous marriage. Once you marry, your estate will change and become more complex, with the issues of community property and joint assets. Also, what happens to your children if you should die? Oh, my, there's a morbid thought! Sorry about that! However, as depressing as that is to think about, especially when you're in the throes of planning your awesome wedding, it's still smart to do so.

Here's another question: what happens if your new spouse dies? What if he hasn't legally adopted your children, or vice versa? You'll find that, in most states, if your children haven't been legally adopted, they can't inherit your estate unless they have been named in a will as your legal beneficiaries. Your current will probably won't hold up in court, because your assets may now become community property or, at the very least, joint assets will go to your spouse if you die, ignoring the rights of your children altogether.

Your best bet is to meet with an estate attorney, who'll help you draw up a new will, a new living trust (if you have one), and see that other important changes are made, including new designations for life insurance beneficiaries.

Wedding Insurance

There are two kinds of wedding insurance you may want to consider. The first is a rider you can have attached to your existing homeowner's or renter's insurance policy that will protect the value of your wedding gifts. This rider is quite affordable.

The second kind of wedding insurance is offered by Fireman's Fund Insurance Company, although it may also be offered by your own insurance company, so check with them as well. This policy covers lost or stolen gifts, plus any non-refundable expenses in case of a canceled wedding (now that's a *really* depressing thought!). It also covers any retaking of photographs or wedding attire replacements, and provides liability insurance for mishaps that may take place during the ceremony or reception, including an injury to a guest.

Chapter 15

WEDDING TOASTS

Toasts are offered throughout the years on birthdays, wedding anniversaries, at graduation parties, and during many other life celebrations, but toasts never seem as poignant and plentiful as they are for a bride and groom, aka the leading man and lady!

The couple will soon realize that friends and family members are delighted for them and want to toast them every chance they can, from their engagement celebration to their wedding day.

Traditional etiquette is still applied to these toasts, although the wording of the toasts themselves may vary, depending on the formality of the party or celebration.

Engagement Parties

The couple may be honored with several engagement parties, and in each case the party's host is expected to offer a toast. The toast is traditionally offered as soon as all the guests have been served a beverage, preceding the serving of refreshments or a meal. The beverage of choice for one of these affairs seems to be champagne, although contemporary etiquette allows for any alcoholic or non-alcoholic beverage.

Following the toast offered by the party's host, anyone present may offer one as well.

An engagement toast should be touching and poignant, as you'll see by these examples, taken from my book, *Diane Warner's Complete Book of Wedding Showers*:

Traditional

"Ladies and gentlemen, please stand with me as we raise our glasses in a toast to _____ and _____. Congratulations on your engagement. May your lives be filled with joy, good health, and a lifetime of happiness."

Contemporary

"_____ and _____, it is an honor to toast to your engagement. May this be the start of something wonderful, a brand-new life, a beautiful beginning. Here's to a future filled with romance, delight, sharing, laughter, and great adventure, as your love grows with each day."

Classic

"Look down you gods, and on this couple drop a blessed crown."—*William Shakespeare*

Ethnic

Irish: "May you have warm words on a cold evening, a full moon on a dark night, and may you know nothing but happiness from this day forward."

Rehearsal Dinner

The rehearsal dinner is traditionally hosted by the groom's parents, so the traditional first toast has always been offered by the groom's father. In today's contemporary world, however, anyone may host the rehearsal dinner, in which case the dinner's host may offer the first toast, followed by any of the following optional toasts:

- The best man toasts the bride and groom.
- The groom toasts his bride and her parents.
- The bride toasts her groom and his parents.
- The fathers of the bride and of the groom offer toasts, welcoming the bride or groom and their family members into their family.

> *Instead of the best man, the two fathers may offer the first toasts, especially if the rehearsal dinner is being hosted by one or both of them.*

Wedding Reception

The best man is the only person required to offer a toast during the wedding reception, although toasts may also be offered by other relatives and friends. His toast should be the first one offered, however, and is usually given after the meal, if one is served, and before the cake-cutting ceremony.

It's customary for the best man to reminisce a little about his friendship with the groom, relating interesting little stories and bits of humor, but always ending on a serious note.

> *The best man's toast should be delivered with as much poignancy and heartfelt sincerity as possible.*

Example of a Best Man's Toast to the Bride and Groom

"What an honor to be here, _____and _____, to be able to share the joy of this day with you as _____(the groom's) best man. You know, it has been said that success in marriage is much more than finding the right person: it is a matter of being the right person, and I can say without reservation that you are so right for each other. When _____(the groom) was in high school and college, he didn't date very much, at least not that I ever knew. He was very selective, preferring to spend his time on the basketball court or cruising over to the coast in his '56 Chevy that he'd worked so hard to restore, rather than to date someone who didn't meet the high standards he had set for his life's mate.

Then he met you, _____ (the bride), and he was a goner. No more hours on the basketball court, and his cruisin' days were over...and why? Because there was nothing he'd rather be doing than spending time with you. You were the one! In fact, it couldn't be more obvious to everyone in this room that you were meant for each other, meant to spend your lives together. And as you set out together as partners on this journey called marriage, my prayers go with you that every day will be as joyous as this. Here's to you, _____ and _____."

Following the best man's toast, this is the normal sequence of toasts offered:

- The fathers of the bride and groom toast the couple and welcome the bride or groom into the family.
- The groom toasts his bride.
- The bride toasts her groom (optional).
- The maid or matron of honor toasts the bride or the couple.
- The best man (on behalf of the bride and groom) offers a thank-you toast to the bridesmaids.

- Other members of the wedding party offer toasts.
- Finally, any other relatives and friends may toast the couple.

General Rules of Etiquette for Toasting

- Before a toast is offered, the person delivering the toast should wait until all the guests have been served a toasting beverage, whether it's champagne or any other alcoholic or non-alcoholic drink.

- It's considered poor etiquette to rap a spoon against a cup or glass to gain the guests' attention; instead, the toaster should stand with the toasting glass held high until he or she has relative silence. Then, once the toaster starts to speak, everyone should quiet down to hear what the person is saying. If there's a serious problem quieting things down, however, the master of ceremonies or the band director may ask for the guests' attention, or the musicians may play a rousing fanfare as a prelude to the offering of the toasts. It also helps to use a microphone.

- The person delivering the toast should always stand and maintain eye contact with the person(s) being toasted.

- It's best if a toast is composed ahead of time so that nothing is accidentally said that would be embarrassing to the person(s) being toasted. Ideally, the toaster should practice delivering the toast in front of a mirror, avoiding annoying mannerisms, such as jiggling keys in the pocket or saying "you know" between phrases.

- The person(s) being toasted should remain seated and should not lift a toasting glass or sip from a toasting glass after the toast has been delivered.

This is considered very poor etiquette because if you do, you're actually toasting yourself.

∞ Anyone who plans on toasting the couple during the reception should limit the amount of alcohol consumed beforehand.

∞ Other than the officiant, it's never appropriate for a vendor or service provider to offer a toast to the couple.

∞ Avoid cliches, profanities, off-color jokes, or anything depressing (such as a recent death in the family).

∞ If either the bride or groom has been married before, the toaster should never mention the first marriage during the toast.

∞ A wedding toast is usually no longer than three to five minutes.

∞ Don't chew gum during the toast.

I have written a comprehensive book titled *Diane Warner's Complete Book of Wedding Toasts* that includes hundreds of traditional and contemporary toasts, plus special toasts by the best man, the fathers, the groom, and the bride. It also includes:

∞ Toasts with ethnic variations.

∞ Toasts inspired by the classics.

∞ Humorous toasts.

∞ Toasts suitable for second marriages.

∞ Toasts for holiday weddings and anniversaries.

∞ Special toasts, such as one to the bride by her mother.

Chapter 16

GIFTS FROM
THE BRIDE AND GROOM

The bride and groom may or may not decide to give each other wedding gifts; however, according to traditional and contemporary etiquette, they *are* expected to present gifts of appreciation to their attendants, their parents, and all those who volunteered to help out with their wedding.

Gifts for Each Other

Some couples do give each other wedding gifts, in addition to their wedding rings, of course.

Popular Gifts From the Bride to Her Groom

- Gold cuff links or tie tack.
- Engraved gold watch.
- Book of love poems.
- Sterling silver picture frame with the bride's photo.
- Silver belt buckle.

Popular Gifts From the Groom to His Bride

- Diamond or cultured pearl necklace.
- Gold or diamond earrings.
- Gold heart-shaped locket.
- Music box.
- Book of love poems.

Gifts for Attendants, Participants, and Helpers

You should give thank-you gifts to your attendants and every unpaid participant and helper, including guest book attendants, musical performers, reception hosts, amateur florist, photographer, or friends who helped decorate the sites.

Here are gift suggestions for women, men, teenagers, and children.

Gifts for Women

- Jewelry or jewelry box.
- Picture frame.
- Scarf.
- Silver spoon.
- Music box.
- Cologne, perfume, or bath toiletries.
- Italian charm bracelet with one personalized charm.
- Gift certificate from her favorite store, restaurant, or spa.
- Tickets to a theater or concert performance.

Gifts for Men

- Pen/pencil set.
- Wallet.

- Silver or gold business card case.
- Swiss army knife.
- Money clip.
- Travel kit.
- Brush and comb set.
- Cologne or aftershave.
- Comb and brush set.
- Tie clasp or cuff links.
- Box of cigars.
- Gift certificate to his favorite sporting goods store or restaurant.
- Tickets to a sports event or concert performance.

Gifts for Teenagers

- CD player.
- CDs or DVDs.
- Electronic or computer games.
- Sports equipment.
- Wallet with real money.
- Heart-shaped locket.
- Sports attire or memorabilia.
- Gift certificate from his or her favorite sporting goods or clothing store.
- Tickets to a sports event or concert performance.

Gifts for Children

- Stuffed animals.
- Bride doll.
- Charm bracelet.

- ∞ Puzzles.
- ∞ Games.
- ∞ Toy trucks.
- ∞ Electronic or computer games.
- ∞ Plastic jar filled with jelly beans.
- ∞ Cookie jar filled with homemade cookies.
- ∞ Personalized T-shirt.

Gifts for Your Parents

Finally, we come to the most poignant and meaningful gifts of all—those for your parents. Depending on the gifts, they may be presented during the couple's private time with their parents at the end of the reception, or after the couple returns from their honeymoon.

You'll want to choose gifts that will be long-lasting mementos of your special day—preferably touching, sentimental gifts that will bring tears to their eyes. Here are some popular choices:

- ∞ Framed wedding invitation with wide matting signed by both of you.
- ∞ Framed original poem or thank-you note.
- ∞ Wedding memorabilia box or basket. Fill it with keepsakes from the wedding.
- ∞ Decorated videotape storage box, to hold a copy of the videotape of your wedding and reception, or a decorated photo album, to hold the wedding photos.
- ∞ Personalized Christmas ornament.
- ∞ Live *wedding tree*. Purchase a live, potted evergreen tree for your parents to plant in their yard as a remembrance of your wedding day.

Chapter 17

ENCORE WEDDING

This may be your second wedding or your fourth, but that doesn't make it any less exciting. You've found love again and your commitment is strong.

In this chapter, we consider the rules of wedding etiquette as they apply to the unique qualities of an encore wedding. For example, do we include all our children from previous marriages in the ceremony? What if they don't get along with each other? What about the ceremony and reception? Should they be subdued, with only close friends and family members present? Or, is it all right to plan a big production, with all the bells and whistles?

Here are a few basic guidelines as you begin to think about your encore wedding:

- Of all weddings today, 30 percent are encore weddings, so you shouldn't feel uncomfortable planning any kind of ceremony and reception you would like. You're in good company!

- Plan a wedding that's unique—try to stay away from any elements of your previous weddings, except for the members of your wedding party, which may be the same.

However, don't get married in the same church as you did the first time, and choose bridesmaids' attire that's as far as possible from your previous weddings. And, of course, *never* wear the same wedding gown as you did before—although that's a no-brainer, right? Get married with different rings. Plan a honeymoon at a different destination. You get the idea!

∞ Keep your sense of humor as you plan this joyous occasion. You're a little older and wiser this time, so relax and have fun. Laughter will be your salvation!

Announcing Your Engagement

Announcing your engagement will follow the same guidelines as your first marriage, except that certain people in your lives should be told first.

Tell Your Children First

It's very important to tell your children first. The worst thing that can happen is for them to hear the news from someone else. Your children may feel threatened by this news, fearing they'll lose your love and be relegated to second place in your life, so reassure them of your love. Follow up the announcement with exciting ways you plan to include them in your wedding.

> Tell each child separately, one after the other, on the same day. You don't want one of your children to tell a sibling before you've had a chance to do so. If—heaven forbid!—your children don't approve of your engagement, hope and pray your fiancé wins them over before the wedding. If this doesn't happen, don't hesitate to schedule a few sessions with a Marriage and Family Therapist (MFT), who'll be able to help.

Tell Your Ex-Spouse

The next person to be informed is your ex-spouse, particularly if he or she is the parent of your children. If you had no children together, it's still a good idea for the ex-spouse to hear the news from you instead of from someone else.

Also, it's important to tell your ex in person, if you can possibly arrange it. In any case, tell him or her in private—not in front of the children.

Tell Your Parents

Tell your parents in person and tell each set of parents separately. (Your fiancé should tell his parents in private, and you should do likewise.)

Tell Your Other Relatives and Friends

Tell them in person or with a telephone call. If you can't reach all of them within a reasonable length of time, send notes. Your goal is to be sure they all hear the news within the same general period of time.

Newspaper Announcements

Although encore wedding engagement announcements are not usually sent to the local newspaper, there's no rule of etiquette that forbids it. So, if you would like your engagement announced, follow the same general procedure described in Chapter 1 regarding newspaper announcements, with these two differences:

- ∞ You'll probably be announcing your own engagement, instead of your parents doing so. However, it's perfectly acceptable for the bride's or groom's parents to announce the engagement if they would like. It will depend on who plans to host the wedding. Because most encore weddings are planned and paid for by the couple themselves, the couple will probably announce their own engagement.

- ∞ If there are children from previous marriages, they may be included in the announcement. They may also be mentioned as being members of your wedding party. For example, your daughter may serve as flower girl and your fiancé's son may serve as ring bearer. The bride's children may walk her down the aisle or the groom's older son may serve as his best man. It's nice to include the children every way possible, beginning with the engagement announcement.

Here's sample wording when the couple and their children announce the engagement together:

Estelle Anne Jameson and Thomas Robert Edmonds,
along with their children, Bianca, Joel, and Patrice,
announce their engagement to marry.
(And so forth.)

Applying the Rules of Etiquette to Your Encore Wedding Plans

One wonderful thing about an encore wedding is that, this time, it's *your* wedding. Not your mother's. Not your friends'. You've been there, done that. This time it's *your* turn to plan the kind of wedding you and your fiancé envision. You're probably paying for the wedding yourselves, which makes it even easier to stand up for what you want.

Here are a few helpful guidelines:

- ∞ Choose a style and ambience that will make this wedding as poignant and meaningful as possible, whether it's an afternoon garden wedding, or an evening candlelight wedding in a quaint chapel.

- ∞ The bride's gown may be white, if she likes; however, it's considered in poor taste for the bride to wear a veil or a long train. If an encore bride decides to wear a veil anyway, it should not cover her face.

- ∞ If you plan to involve your children in your ceremony, choose a time for your ceremony when they will feel rested.

- ∞ Plan a wedding within your budget—don't bog yourselves down with credit card bills to pay off after the honeymoon.

- ∞ Even though you and your fiancé may have plenty of worldly goods left over from your first marriages, and you don't want your guests to feel obligated to bring wedding gifts, it's considered poor taste to say so. In fact, go ahead and establish gift registries, although you'll probably want to register for less traditional gifts, such as camping gear or artwork from a gallery. Do *not* print the words "No gifts please" at the bottom of your wedding invitations—a mega no-no.

- If a friend or relative would like to host a bridal shower or co-ed party for you, that's fine. However, if the bride's friends and family members hosted several bridal showers the first time around, they shouldn't be expected to do so again. If they would like to host an engagement party, however, that would be in great taste.

- Invite anyone you'd like to your wedding, whether they were guests at your first wedding or not. You've been given a second chance at happiness, and you want to share your joy with those closest to you.

- If only one of you was married before, be sensitive to the desires of the first-time bride or groom. Even though it may be a bride's second marriage, her groom may have his heart set on a traditional ceremony and reception, so talk things over before you make any major planning decisions.

> *Wedding guests who gave you gifts the first time around shouldn't be expected to purchase gifts again, although many of them will anyway.*

Degree of Formality

Your wedding may be as formal or informal as you would like, although statistics show that most encore weddings are less formal and much less expensive than first weddings.

Financing the Wedding

The encore bride and groom usually pay for all their wedding expenses, although their parents or other family members may want to help out, especially by donating services or supplies. The important thing is to plan a wedding you can afford, so that you don't start off your new life together owing a pile of money.

> In the United States, a second marriage averages about $10,000 less than a first wedding, so expect to pay no more than $12,000 for everything. See my book, *How to Have a Big Wedding on a Small Budget, 4th Edition,* for second wedding trends and ideas, including ways to trim expenses for a second marriage.

Wedding Invitations

An encore wedding invitation may differ only slightly from a first-time wedding invitation. The two biggest differences will probably be that it isn't as formal as the first time, plus your children may cohost the wedding.

Example of an Invitation to a Wedding Hosted by the Couple Themselves

Our joy will be more complete
if you can share in the celebration
of our marriage
Saturday, the fifth of May
at two o'clock in the afternoon
at
Chapel on the Green
223 Western Avenue
Los Angeles, California
followed by a reception
at
Cambridge House Restaurant
2501 Harrington Street
Audrey Brogue and Trevor Jessup

Example of an Invitation to a Wedding Cohosted by the Couple's Children

Beth Anne Jackson and William Thomson
together with their children
request the honour of your presence at
their wedding
on
Saturday, September 28
at one o'clock
United Methodist Church
227 East Lawn Drive
R.S.V.P. 555-6692

or

Beth Anne Jackson and William Thomson
together with their children
Ashley, Burke, and Justin
request the honour of your presence at
their wedding
(and so on)

Example of an Invitation to a Casual Encore Wedding

Dear Tom and Estelle,

We're getting married on board Cindy's parents' houseboat on Saturday, July 17th at 1 p.m. We hope you'll be able to join us for the celebration, followed by a barbecue lunch.

Call to R.S.V.P. and we'll tell you how to get there.

With love from both of us,

Cindy and Jim

*Example of an Invitation to a Wedding Reception Only
(Following a Private Ceremony)*

The pleasure of your company
is requested
at the wedding reception
for
Roberta Anne Hayes
and
Duane John Harris
on Saturday, October 30
at two o'clock
at Cartridge Country Club
1201 South Broadway Avenue

In your reception invitation, it's not necessary to explain that you are being married in a small private ceremony prior to the reception. The guests will get the message as soon as you arrive from your ceremony site.

Special Touches for an Encore Wedding

Encore brides and grooms like to add special touches to their ceremony and reception, including personalized vows and the inclusion of their children any way they can.

Personalized Vows

I've found that second-time brides and grooms prefer to write their own vows. Most of these couples have been through a lot of heartache and want this wedding to be special in every way.

In my book, *Diane Warner's Complete Book of Wedding Vows*, I include an entire chapter of personalized vows for second marriages. Here is one example:

"_____, God has given us a second chance at happiness, and I praise him for that. I come today to give you my love, to give you my heart, and my hope for our future together. I promise to bring you joy, to be at home with your spirit, and to learn to love you more each day, through all the days of our lives. I promise to be your faithful wife/husband. My love for you is seamless, endless, and eternal."

Receiving Line

If you decide to have one, your receiving line is arranged a little differently than it would be at a first-time marriage:

- ∞ If you have children from a previous marriage, they should be included in the receiving line. You want your children to feel part of the festivities, so have them stand next to you in the line and take the time to introduce each child to each guest who passes through the line.

- ∞ The order is changed from the norm (see Chapter 13) by having the bride and groom first in line, followed by their parents. The couple's friends may not know the parents, so this arrangement makes it easier for the bride and groom to introduce them to their guests.

Involve Your Children in the Wedding and Reception

Even though your children may be quite young, they are impressionable and you want them to remember your wedding day as one of the happiest of their lives. If your children *want* to be involved (ask them first), here are a few wonderful ways you can involve your children in your plans:

∞ Include your children in your wedding vows. In my book, *Diane Warner's Complete Book of Wedding Vows*, I include several touching examples of vows that include children. Here is one of them, a vow from the groom to his new stepdaughter: "_____, I love your Mommy, and today I've taken her as my wife; but, did you know that I love you dearly as well? I want to be as a father to you, and I invite you into my heart. We will have happy times together, you and your Mommy and I. And with this ring I give you my love." (He slides a ring onto the girl's finger.)

∞ Include your children in a Circle of Acceptance Ceremony. This is a sweet ceremony that takes place in front of the altar. You, your children, and the officiant stand in a circle and hold hands. There are many variations to this ceremony, although the officiant usually addresses the children, saying something like this: "Cindy, Mommy and your new daddy want you to feel accepted into your new family being formed today. They also want your blessing. Do you, Cindy, accept your new family circle?" *Hopefully*, Cindy answers, "Yes."

∞ Another precious ceremony is the Family Medallion Ceremony. The family medallion is a beautiful round medal that has three intertwined circles, symbolizing family love and unity. The first two circles represent the union of the man and woman, and the third circle represents the children who are intertwined in their love. The medal is placed on a chain, forming a necklace, which is placed over each child's neck following the couple's wedding vows.

As the parents place the medallions over the necks of their children, they pledge to love and support their children as they become part their new family unit.

⌘ Order flowers for your children: a boutonniere for your son, and a small wrist corsage for your daughter.

⌘ Be sure your children are invited to the rehearsal and, if they are old enough, the rehearsal dinner as well. Try to plan the rehearsal and dinner as early in the day as possible so they won't get too tired. If they are too young to enjoy the dinner, let them come anyway and stay until they get fussy, along with a babysitter assigned to usher them to another room to play with them or watch a kids' video for the duration of the dinner.

⌘ Depending on the ages of your children, involve them in as many ways as you can during the ceremony and reception. They can serve as flower girl, ring bearer, candlelighters, junior attendants, or, if old enough, as maid of honor or best man. They can also help seat the guests, especially their relatives, and the bride's children may walk their mom down the aisle. Children also enjoy handing out programs, attending the guest book, or handing out favors to the guests during the reception.

⌘ An extra special touch is for the bride and groom to mention their children during any toasts they may offer during the rehearsal dinner or wedding reception. It's important for the children to feel loved, valued, and included in this precious new family unit that is being formed.

∞ When you're planning the seating arrangements for your reception, dedicate a special table for your children and a few of their cousins or friends who may also be in attendance. Decorate their table in some unique way, with personalized balloons or gifts at each designated place setting.

∞ Present your children with personalized gifts to commemorate your wedding day. An engraved bracelet, necklace, or locket would be appropriate for your daughter. An engraved watch or a gold chain or bracelet would be appreciated by your son.

∞ Include your children in your honeymoon plans. You can make arrangements for a two-part honeymoon. The first part can be a private time for the two of you. Then, the children can join you for some family-oriented fun, such as a few days together at Disneyland.

> When the officiant announces you as man and wife, include your children by having them stand beside you during the announcement. You want your children to remember this day as the "day we got married," so the officiant may add, "I would also like to introduce Jennifer and Ashley, part of this beautiful new family created today."

Wedding Jewelry

The trend with encore weddings is to forego the engagement ring and design matching personalized wedding rings. The couple may do whatever they want, of course, with the only caveat being that the groom should *not* present his new bride with his ex-spouse's engagement or wedding ring.

Delicate Encore Wedding Issues

Encore weddings have a few questions that are unique to the circumstances. Here are a few of the most common problems you'll face, and ways to handle them.

Can I Announce Our Engagement and Wear My Engagement Ring Before My Divorce is Final?

No! *Not* cool. If your fiancé has given you an engagement ring before your divorce is final, wear it concealed beneath your clothes on a chain around your neck until everything is final.

What Do I Do About the Name Thing?

Take a look in Chapter 14 where you'll see various options that also apply to second marriages. However, if you were divorced or widowed the first time, you have two additional choices.

In the case of divorce, most brides choose to use their first name, their maiden name as a middle name, and their new husband's last name.

In the case of being a widow, most brides use their first name, their previous husband's last name, and their new husband's last name.

Whatever you decide to do about your new legal name, you may decide to use your previous name in certain cases, especially if your name is well-known in your profession.

> If you enclose an at home card in your invitations (see Chapter 8), you may want to let your guests know of any name change on that card as well. For example, you may say, "Beth Anne Jackson will be changing her name to Beth Anne Thomson following her marriage," or "The bride will retain the name Beth Anne Jackson following her marriage."

Do I Invite My Ex-Spouse and Former In-Laws?

Except in rare cases, it's usually best not to invite your ex to your wedding, especially if your ex is the parent of your children. If your ex is in attendance, that can be confusing to your children, who are getting used to being part of a *new* family unit.

If your ex has remarried and you and your children get along great with both of them, it may work out. Give it a lot of thought before you send that invitation.

If you have a sweet relationship with your former in-laws, and they are supportive of your new marriage, you may want them at your wedding, whether your ex is there or not.

> If you do invite your former in-laws to your wedding, introduce them as your friends, or as your children's grandparents, if applicable. Do not introduce them as, "my former mother-in-law," or "my former brother-in-law," and so on.

Chapter 18

AFTER
THE WEDDING

The wedding is over, so you would think it's time to relax. However, those pesky rules of wedding etiquette still apply to all the happenings that take place after the wedding. The most common of these after-wedding happenings are the afterglow, a morning-after breakfast or brunch, a sightseeing tour for your special out-of-town guests, and a gift-opening party when you return from your honeymoon. There are also a few mundane chores to be handled, such as returning rented items, preserving the bride's gown, mailing the wedding announcements, and sending those inevitable thank-you notes.

Afterglow

An afterglow is an intimate gathering that includes the bride and groom, their immediate families, and any close friends who came from out of town especially for the wedding. This warm get-together is usually hosted by one of the bride's or groom's close relatives or their parent's closest friends. This is a time to *glow* for the guests as they bask in the newfound love and joy of your wedding day.

Snacks or a light meal are usually served in a relaxed, cozy setting, often a private home.

Morning-After Breakfast or Brunch

A morning-after get-together may be as formal as a resort's brunch buffet, or as informal as sausage and waffles on the patio of a private home. It may be hosted by a close relative, friend or neighbor who may have watched you grow up and wants to prolong the euphoria of your wedding day. This is also a special time for you to say your good-byes before leaving on your honeymoon.

If this is an informal affair in someone's backyard, various outdoor activities may be included, such as swimming, volleyball, or badminton.

Hospitality and Dinner for Long-Distance Guests

If you have out-of-towners staying in homes and hotels around town, be sure they aren't forgotten the day after the wedding. They'll appreciate being taken on a tour of the city, including a visit to a museum or historical site.

After playing tour guide, be sure to treat them to a lovely dinner, at a nice restaurant or in someone's home.

> *Unless you and your new husband really think this sounds like fun, you're excused from the dinner for out-of-town guests!*

After-the-Honeymoon Gift-Opening Party

The couple's parents often host a casual party after the honeymoon where the bride and groom open their wedding gifts. Only immediate family members and a few very close friends are usually invited to this party, which may be a simple dessert and coffee get-together or an informal buffet supper.

Return of All Borrowed or Rented Items

All rented wedding attire should be returned immediately, as well as any rented or borrowed items, such as tables, chairs, aisle runner, candelabra, and decorations. Think of it as returning the props used in your hit show.

Preservation of the Bridal Gown

Your bridal gown should be cleaned and stored as soon as possible after the wedding. Take it to a dry cleaners that specializes in cleaning and preserving wedding gowns. Any stains should be pointed out, including makeup, food, dirt, or grass stains along the hemline.

Once the gown has been cleaned, it should be wrapped in acid-free paper and stored in an acid-free box in a cool, dry place.

> Do *not* allow the storage box to be vacuum sealed, because this can actually allow retained moisture that may eventually cause mildew.

Wedding Announcements

Designate someone to be in charge of mailing your wedding announcements one or two days after the wedding.

Newspaper Announcements

The announcement of your wedding should appear in your local newspaper the day after your wedding. However, if you want your wedding photo to appear alongside your announcement, it may not appear until a few weeks after the wedding.

Contact the society editors of all the newspapers you'd like to carry the announcement of your wedding; have the form mailed, e-mailed, or faxed to you before the wedding.

Here's a sample newspaper wedding announcement:

Caroline Moisa and Erik McCafferty were married May 15, 2005 at St. Augustine's Catholic Church. A reception followed at Rottingham Country Club. Dee Ramirez, the bride's sister, served as her matron of honor. Jeff Cranson served as best man. Other honor attendants were Linda Kranz, Ashley Simmons, and Megan Grammond. Father Alberto Jiraldo Lopez was the celebrant. The bride is the daughter of Roberta Henderson Moisa and Peter Eugene Moisa. She is a 2005 graduate of the University of Arizona with a B.A. in Education. She is currently teaching at Del Norte Middle School. The groom is the son of Joanne Louise McCafferty and Matthew William McCafferty. He is a 2004 graduate of Oregon State University with a B.S. in Fisheries and Marine Resources and is currently employed by the state of Colorado. The couple honeymooned on Catalina Island, California.

Writing the Thank-You Notes

As soon as you return from your honeymoon and settle down into some kind of a routine, set a goal of writing three or four thank-you notes every day, with the ultimate goal of having them all written no later than six weeks after the wedding. (*No*, you can't get by with thanking people verbally, and *no*, you do not have one year to write the thank-you notes.)

It's acceptable to write one thank-you note for a group gift—you don't need to write a separate thank-you note to each member of the group.

The thanks must always be personalized and written by hand. Here is sample wording:

> *Dear Aunt Eleanor,*
> *Thank you for coming to our wedding. Your presence made our day extra special.*
> *Richard and I want to thank you for your thoughtful gift. We love the breadmaker. In fact, we make fresh bread several times a week. I think Richard is getting spoiled. Thank you so much.*
> *Your loving niece,*
> *Carol*

If the gift was a cash gift, it's nice to thank the giver for the item you purchased, or plan to purchase, with the money.

It's never acceptable to let someone else help you out by writing your thank-you's for you. You would be surprised how many people recognize your mom's or your sister's handwriting!

Chapter 19

THE HONEYMOON

Proper etiquette not only applies to your wedding, but to your honeymoon as well. Etiquette should be followed when:

- ❧ Paying for your honeymoon.
- ❧ Planning your honeymoon.
- ❧ Traveling to your honeymoon destination.
- ❧ Staying at your honeymoon destination.

Paying for Your Honeymoon

The honeymoon is traditionally paid for by the groom and his parents. However, contemporary etiquette allows for the bride and groom to share this expense. Of course, the groom's parents may want to pick up some of the honeymoon expenses, but they are not obligated to do so.

A popular contemporary twist is for the couple to establish a gift registry at a travel agency. That way, guests may contribute toward the cost of the honeymoon, in lieu of a traditional wedding gift.

Planning the Honeymoon

In years past, the groom was responsible for choosing a honeymoon destination and making all the plans, which were often kept secret from the bride until after the wedding reception. However, in today's contemporary world of honeymoon etiquette, the bride and groom usually make the plans together.

> *If you have children from a previous marriage, you may want to take a look at Chapter 17 for ways to include them in your honeymoon.*

It has become popular to spend the wedding night at a local resort or hotel, delaying the hassle of travel until the next day.

One nice rule of etiquette that still holds true today is that the best man is the person responsible for following through on the honeymoon plans. He's the one who should call to confirm all their reservations, pick up last-minute tickets or travel itineraries from the travel agent, and make sure the couple has everything they need with them on their wedding day, including their passports, hotel and rental car confirmations, ATM cards, money, medications, and so forth.

> *The bride must apply for her passport in her maiden name, which will still be legal once she's married. However, be sure the airline ticket is also in her maiden name because it's imperative that the names on her ticket and passport match.*

Traveling to Your Honeymoon Destination

Modern rules have evolved for honeymoon travelers, mainly due to the increase of thieves and con artists who often take advantage of honeymooners. Here are a few precautions you should take:

- ∞ Watch your luggage carefully. If you're on an airport shuttle, be sure someone doesn't "accidentally" take your luggage with them at their stop. Also, when standing in line at the check-in counter, keep your luggage in *front* of you, so that they are touching your foot. This will make it more difficult for a thief to walk off with your bags.

- ∞ Watch for distractions. For example, a thief may "accidentally" drop his ice-cream cone onto your shoulder or lap, then make a big fuss of cleaning you up with a napkin while an accomplice picks your pocket or walks off with your cell phone. Other ploys are a "mother" who asks you to hold her baby while she rushes back into the plane to retrieve her purse, or a man "suffering a heart attack." Thieves love honeymooners because they know you're probably not paying attention to anything but each other.

- ∞ Be careful when you enter your credit card number on the dial pad of a pay telephone. Shield the pad with your hand. As hard as it is to believe, a thief may have high-powered binoculars trained on the pad so he can steal your credit card number.

- ∞ Keep your valuable airline tickets, travelers checks, credit cards, driver's licenses, and cash in a money belt. A money belt is a little uncomfortable, but worth it.

Staying at Your Honeymoon Destination

Once you reach your destination, here are a few helpful suggestions:

- Tell everyone you're on your honeymoon—you'll be surprised how many freebies this news will bring, from an upgraded hotel room to a complimentary dessert.

- Leave appropriate tips. Here are guidelines:

Airport porter	$1 per bag.
Ship's cabin or dining-room steward	$3 per day, per person.
Hotel bellboy	$1 per bag, plus an extra dollar or two for extra service, such as giving you directions to restaurants.
Doorman	$2 for hailing a taxi.
Waiter or waitress	15 percent of the bill.
Hotel chambermaid	$5 to $10 per week.
Taxi driver	$2 or $3 per trip, plus a little extra if he helps with your luggage or races across town to get you to your destination on time.
Parking attendant	$2 when car delivered.
Golf caddie	25 percent of his fee.
Tour guide/charter-bus driver	$5.

> *Always check to see if a tip has already been included in the cost of the tour, the meal, or any services provided, especially if you're honeymooning in a foreign country.*

Back Home

As you start out your new life together, tradition says that the groom should carry his bride over the threshold of their new home. This tradition began as a superstition that said the groom should lift his bride over the threshold to protect her from evil spirits lurking in the floorboards beneath it. Although it's perfectly proper to forego this tradition, many of today's couples go along with it just for fun.

Chapter 20

MURPHY'S LAW

We all know about Mr. Murphy, that dreaded uninvited guest. He shows up everywhere, even on movie sets! But if he shows up at your wedding or reception, Murphy's Law says that "anything that can go wrong will go wrong," resulting in wedding bloopers.

Here are a few real-life wedding bloopers and what you can do to avoid them at your wedding.

Wedding Blooper #1: Too Much Party Time

The groom and his brother, who served as his best man, partied a little too long and hard at the bachelor party the night before the wedding, so they were really hungover. Their eyes were bloodshot and they could barely stand up, but the worst of it was that when the best man threw up, this triggered the groom to do the same! The bride's gown, plus the carpet in front of the altar, were a mess. The bride's dad quickly grabbed two folding chairs from the side of the sanctuary and placed them under the groom and the best man. Fortunately, they were near the end of the ceremony, so they survived until they could get cleaned up for the reception.

Moral of the Story:

Plan the bachelor party for the weekend before the wedding (not the night before!).

Wedding Blooper #2: Avoiding an X-Rated Reception

We've all seen cases where one or two of the guests had a little too much to drink and became loud and obnoxious. But in this case, the bride's uncle (her father's brother), took advantage of the open bar and had one drink after the other, until he was flushed and could hardly stand. The worst of it was his insistence on grabbing the mike and making toasts that had sexual overtones. He thought he was hilarious, but everyone else, of course, was mortified. Finally, the bride's dad calmly put his arm around his brother's shoulder and walked him outside, eased him into the passenger seat of his car, and drove him home.

Moral of the Story:

First of all, you might give second thoughts to providing an open bar, but, in any case, be aware of any friends or relatives who might tend to drink a little too much during the reception. Assign someone to keep an eye on the person and, if necessary, separate him from the other guests if he becomes disruptive, even if it means calling a cab or driving the person home.

Wedding Blooper #3: A "Well-Done" Hairdo

The bride's mom had a friend who volunteered to do the women's hair for the wedding. She arrived at the church with all her gear, including a new, super-powerful, extra-hot curling iron. She was excited because she said the curling iron would assure that the bride's upswept hairdo would stay in tight curls all day without going limp. The problem was that the woman hadn't used the curling iron before and it burned the bride's hair to the point where one section turned dark orange and became singed and crisp. The only solution was to cut off the damaged hair, which happened to be on top of her head where it would be visible. After lopping off a sizable strand, the stylist compensated by wrapping the rest of the hair around the "thin" section. Fortunately, none of the guests realized what had happened.

Moral of the Story:

Have your hair styled by someone you know, whether the stylist comes to your wedding site or you have your hair done in her salon. If you do decide to have a friend style your hair for your wedding day, practice ahead of time so you'll know what to expect.

Wedding Blooper #4: Fertility vs. Fidelity

As the bride slipped the ring on her groom's finger, she said, "…as a sign of my love and fertility" (instead of "fidelity"). Everyone laughed, of course, including the groom, but the bride's face turned crimson when she realized what she'd said. Of course, being "fertile" isn't a mortal sin, so it wasn't a disastrous blooper.

Moral of the Story:

Practice reciting your vows, including your ring vows, during the week before the wedding. Then, if you should get the wording mixed up, at least you tried! After all, what's a tiny glitch in the overall scheme of things.

Wedding Blooper #5:
The Missing Marriage License

This is the only thing that went wrong at my daughter's wedding. Fortunately, no one ever knew what a panic we were in right before the ceremony. I was with my daughter in a dressing room at the back of the church and the men were gathering in the pastor's study in the front of the church. Suddenly, about a half hour before the ceremony was to start, the pastor knocked at our door. When I opened it, he said that the groom was sure we had the marriage license, and that he couldn't legally perform the ceremony without it. I told him I didn't know anything about it. It turns out that the groom had given my daughter the license for safe-keeping, and she had placed it on top of her desk in her room. So, my husband drove back home (about 15 minutes each way), found the license, and got back in time. I thought the pastor, who was a close personal friend, would perform the ceremony anyway, even if we couldn't find the license, but he said, no, that in the state of California it was illegal for him to perform the ceremony without the license. Whew! That was a close one!

Moral of the Story:

Follow up on all the details, right down to the last minute, even if the responsibility isn't technically yours to worry about. For some reason I never even gave the license a thought and I certainly didn't know it was sitting on my daughter's desk all that time! A word to the wise!

Wedding Blooper #6:
The Best Man Was Out of This World

This is such a common blooper—someone in the wedding party faints. In fact, I have personally seen it happen at least a half dozen times. The main reason why someone faints is because the best man, bridesmaid, or whoever, is stressed and locks up his or her knees. Anyone who stands straight with locked knees for more than 10 minutes is likely to faint, whether you're a soldier standing at attention, or a choir member waiting to perform. Another cause of fainting is that the room is hot and there is poor ventilation.

Moral of the Story:

Never lock your knees when standing (alternate your weight from one leg to the other, always keeping one knee bent), and if it's a warm day, open the windows or place floor fans directed toward the members of the wedding party. This blooper is one of the easiest to prevent.

Wedding Blooper #7:
The "Adorable" Ring Bearer

The bride's three-year-old nephew served as ring bearer. He did fine until the couple was reciting their vows and he evidently realized he had messed his pants. So, he kept reaching down inside his little tuxedo slacks, then he'd bring his finger to his nose and smell it. Evidently, it didn't smell too good because he made an awful face which, of course, caused the guests to laugh right in the middle of the vows! We've all witnessed the humorous antics of a flower girl or a ring bearer, from singing "Jesus Loves Me" loudly during the ceremony, to lying down in front of the altar to take a little nap.

Moral of the Story:

Even though you think it would be adorable to have a young relative serve as flower girl or ring bearer, take a firm stand that no one under four years old will participate.

Wedding Blooper #8: Just Wing It

The groom's brother, who was serving as best man, placed the ring carefully on top of his dresser for safekeeping. However, right before the ceremony was to begin, he realized he had forgotten it, and he lived too far from the ceremony site to retrieve it in time, so the matron of honor loaned her wedding ring for the ceremony.

Moral of the Story:

To prevent this type of blooper, someone needs to call the best man the morning of the wedding, to be sure he has placed the ring safely in his jacket pocket. If he forgets the ring in spite of all the reminders, don't panic. The groom can either pretend he's sliding a ring on his bride's finger, or he can borrow someone else's wedding ring to use for the ring ceremony, to be replaced with the real thing as soon as possible.

Let's hope and pray your wedding is blooper-free! Meanwhile, just remember that it all comes down to this: if you can say that you're husband and wife by the end of the day, it's been a *great* wedding day, in spite of Mr. Murphy's visit!

CONCLUSION

I'm often asked, of all the weddings I've attended or helped plan, which ones are my favorites. That is an impossible question, because I love every bride and groom, and I'm crazy about weddings in general. However, if I were pressed, I would have to say that my favorite weddings are those with these qualities:

- An abundance of good taste.
- No one's feelings are hurt.
- No one has been exploited or "used."
- A poignant, sacred ceremony, with no jokes, no silliness, no suggestive attire, and where the vows are taken seriously. (I think the reception is a better venue for the fun and silliness.)
- A warm, joyous reception where all the guests feel welcome, the toasts are tasteful, and a minimum amount of alcohol is consumed. Also, and this is just my personal opinion, I prefer a reception that does away with the *cake smash* (where the bride and groom smash cake into each other's faces).

Follow Your Heart and Do What Seems Right to You

You'll remember in my Introduction, I compared the rules of wedding etiquette to the rules of golf. Each of these games must be played by the rules. However, when it comes to your wedding, you have the right to abide by the rules, bend the rules, or do away with them altogether!

After all, even though professional golfers are obligated to follow the stringent rules of golf, no one says they can't play with their favorite brand of golf clubs, or wear any color shirt they like. I even know of one player who has a talking tiger in his bag!

I hope your wedding day is wonderful in every way.

Index

ABOUT THE AUTHOR

Diane Warner is the best-selling author of 22 books, including *Complete Book of Wedding Vows*, *Big Wedding on a Small Budget*, *Complete Book of Wedding Showers*, and *Complete Book of Wedding Toasts*. She also writes for magazines and newspapers, such as *Bottom Line*, *New York Daily News*, *Washington Weddings*, and *BJ's Journal*, plus Websites, including *dreamweavers.com* and *theweddingshow.net*. She speaks professionally, conducts seminars, and is a frequent guest on radio talk shows, as well as national TV, including CNN, Home and Garden network, and the Discovery Channel.

Diane attended UCLA on a Theatre Arts scholarship, and is a past member and officer with NSA (National Speakers Association). She lives with her author husband, Jack, in Tucson, Arizona. They have two grown children, four grandchildren, and enjoy playing golf and singing in a touring choir sponsored by their church. Visit Diane at her Website, *dianewarnerbooks.com*.

OTHER BOOKS
BY DIANE WARNER

Career Press

Complete Book of Wedding Vows
Complete Book of Wedding Toasts
Complete Book of Wedding Showers
Complete Book of Baby Showers
Diane Warner's Wedding Question & Answer Book
Best Wedding Ever

New Page Books

Diane Warner's Big Book of Parties
Diane Warner's Complete Book of Children's Parties
Diane Warner's Great Parties on Small Budgets

For Dummies, John Wiley Publishing

Single Parenting for Dummies, co-authored with Marion Peterson

F & W Publications

How to Have a Fabulous,
  Romantic Honeymoon on a Budget
How to Have a Great Retirement on a Limited Budget

Betterway Books

How to Have a Big Wedding on a Small Budget, 4th edition
Beautiful Wedding Decorations and Gifts on a Small Budget
Picture-Perfect, Worry Free Weddings

Writer's Digest Books

Big Wedding on a Small Budget Planner and Organizer

Penton Overseas, Inc.

The Perfect Wedding Planner

Jist Works
(co-authored with her husband, Jack, and Clyde Bryan):

The Inside Secrets of Finding a Teaching Job, 2nd Edition

Jist Publishing
(co-authored with her husband, Jack, and Clyde Bryan):

The Unauthorized Teacher's Survival Guide, 2nd Edition

Cook Communications

Puppets Help Teach
Puppet Scripts for Busy Teachers

Visit Diane at her Website, *dianewarnerbooks.com*, where you can read excerpts and find out more about her books